# What You Do Best

## IN THE
## *Body of Christ*

### Discover Your Spiritual Gifts, Personal Style, and God-Given Passion

# BRUCE BUGBEE

ZondervanPublishingHouse

*Grand Rapids, Michigan*

*A Division of* HarperCollins*Publishers*

**WILLOW CREEK**

**RESOURCES**

*Helping People Become
Fully Devoted to Christ*

*What You Do Best*
Copyright © 1995 by Bruce Bugbee

Requests for information should be addressed to:

📖 ZondervanPublishingHouse
*Grand Rapids, Michigan 49530*

---

**Library of Congress Cataloging-in-Publication Data**

Bugbee, Bruce.
    What you do best : in the body of Christ / Bruce Bugbee.
       p.    cm.
    ISBN: 0-310-49431-1 (pbk.)
    1.Gifts, Spiritual.  2. Lay ministry.  3. Pastoral theology.  I. Title
BT767.3.B84     1995
253—dc 20                                     95-37469
                                                 CIP

---

*Edited by Rachel Boers*
*Interior design by Joe Vriend*

*Printed in the United States of America*

---

02 /DC/ 20 19 18

# Contents

*To the children of divorce*

# Acknowledgments

This is a book about biblical community. My understanding of the church has been the result of a journey through many congregations who have shaped my theology and ministry. They have been patient and gracious with my participation and the development of the concepts shared in this book. I want to thank the following churches for their ministry to me: The Crystal Cathedral (Garden Grove, CA), Calvary Chapel (Costa Mesa, CA), El Montecito Presbyterian Church (Montecito, CA), Pasadena Covenant Church (Pasadena, CA), Christ Community Church (Buena Park, CA), First Reformed Church (Orange City, IA), Willow Creek Community Church (South Barrington, IL), and South Coast Community Church (Irvine, CA).

My relationship and ministry with Bill Hybels and Don Cousins through the years have generated additional insights for the application of these principles in churches around the world. As my coauthors of *Network: The Right People ... In the Right Places ... For the Right Reasons,* their ministries continue to be a witness to the building of biblical communities.

I thank my friend Jim Mellado of the Willow Creek Association for his support and commitment to the contents of these materials. He has demonstrated the teachability and life-changing potential of them with different groups through the years.

Wendy Guthrie provided the iron-sharpens-iron relationship for forging the ideas into a simple and crisp presentation. She is loved for her patience and ability to be "ruthlessly gracious" with me.

Jack Kuhatschek, Rachel Boers, Lela Gilbert, and Luanna Young made contributions to the manuscript. They have provided a much more readable text that will serve the reader well. I have appreciated their support throughout the process.

Most authors acknowledge the sacrifice their family made to make the book possible. As I complete this project, I am very aware of the contribution they made when they gave up valuable family time. Thank you Valerie, Brittany, Brianne, Bronwyn, and Todd. You are loved!

# Introduction

I believe God has been changing the hearts of his people. Today, believers are beginning to actively pursue their roles of service in and through the local church. Historically, serving hasn't sold. But we are seeing the beginning of a new era.

The Holy Spirit is moving throughout his church, crossing denominational lines and geographical boundaries. He is energizing a worldwide wave with little respect for theological or doctrinal differences. God is uniting his people today around his purpose for the church: To glorify God and to edify others.

Biblical teaching on spiritual gifts is inspiring universal interest among churches. Church leaders are supposed to equip the saints for the work of ministry—a biblical concept that is easy to understand but difficult to implement. Churches have been wanting the priesthood of all believers to be evident in their congregations, but that has been more teaching than action. One question bringing the church together is: "How do we get the right people in the right places for the right reasons?"

*What You Do Best* presents the vision and values for a ministry to do just that! This book can help you develop yourself—and God's people—for ministry. Its approach is different because it starts with a personalized process built on the belief that each individual is unique, with different passions, spiritual gifts, and personal styles. When you are serving in your area of passion, you will serve more enthusiastically. When using your spiritual gifts, you will serve more competently. When serving in ways that are consistent with your personal style, you will serve with greater freedom.

I have written for average believers who have committed their lives to Jesus Christ, and who, since doing so, have felt like something is still missing in their Christian experience. They do not seem to have found sustaining joy, meaning, and purpose. They have sat in the pews, listened to the messages, put money in the baskets, and still have not been able to find where they can make their unique contribution in a meaningful place of service. They know they should serve—they really *want* to serve. But they are not sure how to best serve because most of the time their efforts in service have not resulted in pleasant experiences. Does this describe you?

This book is a message of hope that will take you beyond the "should" and "ought" to the "who" and "how." *What You Do Best* will guide you to consider the biblical community that God intended the church to be by helping you identify and express your unique contribution as an integral part of the body of Christ. You are needed in the church—not because there are slots to fill, but because in and through your ministry, God's grace is released and his purposes are fulfilled.

*You* are the subject of this book. It will cause you to examine yourself, assess your growth, and reflect on your relationship with Jesus Christ. Read it at a pace that allows you to do what you need to do to personally benefit from it.

I place a high value on the local church as the means that God has chosen to reach the world. I don't see any other plan. The local church is his church—the bride of Christ—that is to be presented pure and without blame. So, without apology, I am committed to building up the ministries of local churches (para-church ministries and community involvement have validity, but they have not been the primary focus of my writing here).

While I am committed to the local church, I am aware that some churches have impersonal, controlling, and argumentative environments. Personal agendas have destroyed much of the church's unity and effectiveness. Power and position have replaced prayer and submission. Some readers may be Christians who have given up on the local church. They gather with friends and attend a few studies, but they have no interest in the local church. Sadly, I understand where they are coming from.

With hope, I present to you a new vision for the church. There are growing numbers of believers, leaders, and churches cooperating with the Holy Spirit in developing biblical communities. They are springing up everywhere. Once you discover your role in the church, together we can create ministries that will cause a skeptical and unbelieving world to stop and say, "There must be a God; look at how those people love one another!" It starts with you, within your heart. Pray that God's work will first be done in you so that his work might be done through you.

It is my hope that you will share the concepts in *What You Do Best* with others. Its message is freeing God's people to pursue their ministry calling with enthusiasm and confidence. Talk about it. Study it in depth together. As you work through it in groups, you will emerge from the process with a greater understanding of the church and your role within it. Your life and ministry will have greater meaning and impact.

I am more amazed than anyone at how God is using these concepts to impact thousands of people in hundreds of churches around the world. It has happened one life at a time. One church at a time. His grace is amazing! Mother Teresa once said, "I am a pencil in the hand of God." I trust you will see his fingerprints as you read. I consider it a privilege to be able to serve you with this message. Enjoy!

NOW THE BODY IS NOT MADE UP OF ONE PART BUT OF MANY. IF THE WHOLE BODYWERE  AN EAR WHERE WOULD THE SENSE OF SMELL BE? THE HEAD CANNOT SAY TO THE FEET, "I DON'T NEED YOU!" THE EYE CANNOT  SAY TO THE HAND, "I DON'T NEED YOU!"

## Chapter One

# Does God Have a Purpose for My Life— Really?

I never thought it would happen. But it did. It was a dream come true. We designed and built our own home!

My wife and I were both raised in southern California. Then, after nearly thirty years, we moved to a small town in northwest Iowa. Among many special friendships was one with a carpenter named Gary. Before long, with his help, we were actually considering the possibility of building a new home. We explored costs. We purchased a lot. We agreed on a design. We built the house, and we moved in just in time for Thanksgiving.

While in the Midwest, I discovered that there really are four seasons. Following the snowy winter came spring showers, and it was time to landscape our new home. We went to the nursery and bought trees, shrubs, and flowers. We planted the lawn and the yard was set.

While most of our plants did really well, some died. I went back to the nursery and got more. I planted them. They died too. One afternoon I was in the yard explaining to my neighbor (actually complaining about) how frustrated I was with my plants. I showed him how some of them were doing really well while others kept dying.

He made a brilliant observation. He said, "These plants won't grow here!" (At that point, I figured he must be a college graduate. He was able, so graphically, to articulate the obvious.)

I said, "Really?"

He went on to explain. "These plants require direct sunlight. Have you ever noticed that the sun never shines within three feet of the north side of your house? They should be placed where they can get the sunlight they need to grow."

It seemed so simple. Yet someone had to explain to me how God had made each plant with different requirements. A plant needing direct sun will perish or flourish, depending on the amount of sun it receives. Another plant, requiring shade, will have its potential destroyed in direct sunlight. When I understood what the plants needed, it was not difficult to find an appropriate place for them.

So, the "bad" plants I had purchased were not really bad at all. They were simply planted in the wrong place. In short, I had learned two important and related gardening lessons: First, know what a plant needs to flourish. Second, place it in the appropriate environment.

## Created with a Purpose in Mind

In my twenty-five years of ministry, I've discovered that many people have had similar experiences in their lives. Like poorly planted shrubs, they often feel misplaced. Maybe you've felt that way too. Take a moment to check the statements below that apply to you:

_____ I feel that I am capable of accomplishing more than I am presently achieving.

_____ I sense that God wants to use me in a meaningful way, but I'm not sure how.

_____ My frustration and confusion about not knowing just what to do makes me less confident and competent.

_____ I desire to be more fruitful and fulfilled, making a difference with my life.

_____ I feel there must be something wrong with me because I still have not been able to figure out what I should be doing.

_____ I wish I knew God's will for my life.

_____ I am often asked to do things I am not interested in doing.

If you checked any or all of the statements above, then this book is for you. In the pages that follow, you will find some practical insights and helpful tools to assist you in two of the most important aspects of your life: Identifying the particular person God has made you to be; and discovering how you can be fruitful and fulfilled in a meaningful place of service.

Are you in an environment that is enabling you to realize your greatest potential? Maybe like the plant, you are not a bad Christian, but you are unaware of what you need, and you aren't sure of the appropriate position from which your life could make an impact on others.

At times, I have felt that there was something wrong with me because I was not growing or developing in ways that those around me expected. Have you heard the saying, "Bloom where you are planted"? What happens when you aren't blooming? There must be something wrong with you—right? No, not necessarily.

God has created and designed us with a purpose in mind. We are "wired" to care about some things more than others. We have been given a passion. We have been given spiritual gifts to competently accomplish ministry tasks. We have also been designed with a personal style of relating to others and the world around us.

When you know your God-given passion, spiritual gifts, and personal style, then you'll know what you need to be both fruitful and fulfilled in your life and ministry.

## The Tension

Most of us know that we should serve God. We know that God not only desires, but commands us to serve (Galatians 5:13). And we want to obey. We have a genuine desire to honor him by fulfilling his purposes and plans for our lives. But many of us don't know how to serve. While we want to serve and know we *should* serve, it has been difficult to find the places where we are able to make our unique contributions. Rather than constantly "replanting" ourselves in a variety of environments in the hope that we might find fulfillment and fruitfulness, doesn't it make sense to discover what God created us for in the first place?

You can gain a better understanding of what your contribution should be through the identification of your servant profile, which you'll find throughout the coming chapters. Your servant profile indicates those three keys that we mentioned before: your God-given passion, your spiritual gifts, and your personal style. With an understanding of your servant profile, you can increase your ability to follow God's will for your life.

You may believe the common notion that God's will for your life is sealed in a mysterious time capsule somewhere, only to be found by those who attend the greatest number of seminars, prayer meetings, Sunday school classes, outreach events, camps, worship services, and conferences. Fortunately, it is more likely that God's will is revealed through his unique design of the person he made you to be.

## No One Ever Asked

We were sitting in a room, just the three of us. Nancy and I were talking with Sarah about her servant profile and what she might be sensing God was leading her to do. Nancy and Sarah had been in the same church and had known each other for years. In fact, Nancy did not think getting together was really necessary, because she already knew just about everything there was to know about Sarah.

During the conversation, Sarah mentioned that she had a passion to tutor children who were having difficulties or who were needing to learn English as a second language. Nancy was silent for a moment. Then she sat back in her chair, and in a bewildered voice she asked Sarah why she had never mentioned this passion. Sarah reflected for a moment and said, "No one ever asked me before what I wanted to do."

I will never forget that moment. How sad to think of the many years Sarah had not felt confident enough to make her contribution. I felt angry that, although the church had many programs, there were so few that empowered the passions and gifts of God's people into expression. There was joy in the air as we considered the possibilities of Sarah's desire being fulfilled. All she needed was a room, a light, and permission, and she could become a caring tutor.

## From Ministry Impact to Marketplace Success

Learning about our passion, gifts, and style can help us both in ministry and in the marketplace. When I met Jim, he was committed to excellence. He was a hard-working professional who always wanted to be his best. He often struggled in the church, where it seemed to him that similar values were not demonstrated. Jim saw the church as slow, cumbersome, and often out of touch with the realities and pressures that he regularly faced in his life. It was his hope that he would be able to make a meaningful contribution that would be appreciated.

Jim was quite eager to learn. He grew in his understanding of his servant profile and began applying it to his life. Eventually, Jim joined my ministry team and we served together for several years. During that time, Jim became an articulate communicator and served as a trainer. His passion for organizational excellence enabled him to focus on getting the right people in the right places for the right reasons within the ministries of the church. He sharpened his gifts and was able to see the fruit of his ministry. He had the satisfaction of knowing that his contribution was making a difference in the lives of many people as well as in building up the local church.

The marketplace held many challenges for Jim too. After learning about his own profile, he started looking at the people he worked with in terms of their passion, gifts, and style, and began to make some changes in the way he organized personnel in his office. The people in his office became more productive in less time. They experienced more ownership in the work because they better understood their contribution to the team. As a result, Jim is an often-sought leader who is pursued because of his effectiveness in getting positive results.

When you know who God has created you to be and you begin to express it faithfully, both your professional life and your personal ministry will take on new levels of purpose and meaning. It starts when your ministry impact is affirmed by those you serve in the church. Those truths, then taken into the broader areas of your life, can expand your purpose and value.

## Assumptions About You

Before we move on to your personal profile, I want you to know that I am making some assumptions. We all do. Here's what I assume to be true:

First, I am speaking to those who call themselves Christians. But even if you have not come to the place where you have personally committed your life to Jesus Christ, you should certainly keep reading. Just bear in mind that, while most of these thoughts will apply to everyone, they have been primarily directed to believers pursuing their purpose in the ministry of Jesus Christ.

Second, I am assuming that you are sincerely seeking the truth. As you read, pray that you will be open to the voice of the Holy Spirit. Some of your present thoughts and perceptions about the church, ministry, or yourself may be challenged. I hope you will attempt to make honest evaluations and that you are willing to rethink and explore what you need to in order to uncover God's purpose for your life.

Third, I assume that you are not continuing to walk with unrepentant sin or broken and unreconciled relationships in your life. If you are not appropriately relating to God and others, it will be difficult to hear what you may need to hear. God's grace is necessary to turn anger, bitterness, and a rebellious heart into love, forgiveness, and a caring heart.

## Make a Commitment

Does God have a purpose for your life—really? Yes, he does. Can you know what it is? Yes, you can! You can discover both your purpose and where you can make your unique contribution.

Take a minute now to consider our journey and the path we will be taking. It will require more than just reading; the real benefits of this book will come as you do personal reflection along the way. Make a commitment to

- Pray to hear the voice of the Holy Spirit and to obey willingly.
- Seek to develop a deeper relationship with Jesus Christ.
- Assess the passion God has put on your heart to make a caring difference.
- Identify your spiritual gift to accomplish God's work God's way.
- Evaluate your personal style as God's means of relating to others.
- Submit yourself to honestly pursue God's purpose for your life.
- Participate according to your servant profile, in order to be fruitful and fulfilled as you glorify God and edify others.

Lord,
    I really want to make a difference,
but I'm not sure how to do it.
    Please give me the wisdom to know
who you want me to be and
    where I can best make a contribution.
Reveal to me my passion,
    my spiritual gifts, and
my personal style.
    Most of all, give me a servant's heart.
Help me to seek your will and authority,
    to have peace with my past, and
to have confidence about my future.
    I want to follow the example you've set for me.
Help me fulfill the special purpose
    you've designed me for.
In Jesus' name,
    Amen.

## Chapter Two

# Who Does God Say That I Am?

When we were children, some of us liked to color. Others liked to cut and paste. I liked to connect the dots. There was a kind of mystery and intrigue to this activity. Before starting, I would stare at the dots (and sometimes they included a few lines) to see if I could make out the figure they concealed. Usually I could not. Then, pencil in hand, I drew a line from dot to dot, and the image slowly appeared. What I was not able to see at first, soon became clear. Once I knew what it was, it seemed to be very obvious.

Connecting dots can be quite informative. Try this. See if you can connect these nine dots with four straight lines without lifting your pen or pencil from the paper. Take a minute (or several) to try this.

```
1       2       3
•       •       •

4       5       6
•       •       •

7       8       9
•       •       •
```

Don't give up! It really can be done. Try once more.

Now, before you continue reading, I'll show you how it can be done. Start at the first dot and make the first straight line moving down through dots four and seven and going beyond to where dot ten might be. From that point, draw the second straight line through dots eight and six to another imaginary dot to the right of dot three. From there, the third straight line is made back to dot one through dots three and two. The fourth and final line is made from dot one through dot five, ending at dot nine.

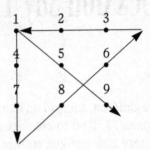

When most people see this exercise for the first time, they cannot figure out how to connect the dots. When shown, they say they didn't know you could go "outside the box," or "outside the lines." What box? What lines?

Interestingly, when it comes to other aspects of their lives, people often do the same thing—they create boundaries or rules that keep them from accomplishing what they are trying to do. When we're seeking growth, we need to be open to the possibility that the rules we have adopted about who we are may be different than what is actually true. Our perspective, grid, or paradigm defines the way we hear and view those around us. The good news is we can enlarge that perspective to see things from God's viewpoint—seeing as God sees (Philippians 2:5).

## In Search of New Perspectives

People saw Peter as a fisherman. Jesus saw him as a fisher of men.

People saw Saul as a persecutor of the church. God saw Paul (Saul) as an ambassador for the church.

People saw David as a shepherd of sheep. God saw David as a shepherd of his people.

How do people see you? How do you see yourself? How does God see you?

"The Lord does not look at the things man looks at. Man looks at the outward appearance, but the Lord looks at the heart" (1 Samuel 16:7). For most of us, seeing as God sees requires a new way of thinking. Some of the perceptions we have of God, the church, and who we are will not help us to find our unique ministry contribution. We need new understanding and descriptions. Finding a clear biblical perspective will help us review both the purpose of the church and our unique role within it.

As we discuss different issues, I challenge you to consider and reconsider the material I'm presenting. Pray about it. Discuss it with others. Listen to what they say, to what they see, and to what God is revealing to you. We need his help to see as he sees. We need to seek out a more encompassing perspective of God's will for us and for his church.

## See the Woman?

A different perspective can entirely change what we see. I was sitting in class one day when the professor put the following picture on the overhead projector. He asked us to describe the woman we saw in the picture.

One student began describing a woman in her midtwenties. She was looking away from us. She had a classy appearance and was wearing a necklace and a fancy hat with a feather.

I was confused. The woman that I was looking at had to be at least eighty years old. She had witchlike features, with a big nose and pointed chin. Instead of looking away, she was looking downward.

The class was divided between those who saw an old woman and those who saw a young woman. After some debate, a representative from each side went forward to trace what they saw. Both women were in the same picture! (Can you see both of them?) There were many "Ohs" and "Ahs," but even after each woman's features were pointed out, some students still could see only what they first recognized.

I have seen this picture used many times since, and the results are always the same. Some see a young woman. Some see an old woman. Few are able to see both without being shown. Why? Because what we first see sets the pattern we focus on. Breaking that pattern is difficult. It can be done, but most of us need help.

## Who Is the Minister?

Let's move on to another familiar image. What picture forms in your mind when you think of a minister? Is it someone wearing a robe who preaches at the front of a church? Is it someone who visits old people in the hospital? Is it someone who knows Greek and Hebrew? Do you think of a reverend, a pastor, or a priest? Would you describe a minister as someone who is paid to run the church and lets you know if he or she needs something? As you envision a minister, do you see yourself? Look at it this way: You are a minister; therefore, you have a ministry.

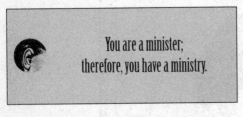

You are a minister; therefore, you have a ministry.

You might not know yet what your ministry is. You may not know how to minister. But you are a minister if you are a follower of Christ. God has created you, a new person in Christ, to fulfill some specific ministry needs.

Many people are confused about what it means to be a minister because they have defined *minister* by the traditional models they have seen. Some of these are very limiting models that have kept many of God's people outside the picture. To ask these people to become involved in ministry is to ask them to step outside their "ministry box." They may not be comfortable. They may not feel they have permission to serve in ways that do not fit the picture of ministry that they've always held in their minds.

What about you? New possibilities for the church will emerge as you better understand who God has created you to be. Once you are making your unique contribution in a meaningful place of ministry, previously unmet needs will be met. It bears repeating: You are a minister. Does that idea confuse you? Before we go on, perhaps we need to talk about what a minister really is.

For centuries, the pastor was the educated, paid professional who ministered to God's people. He was responsible for the ministry, while the congregation helped him do his ministry and financially supported it. Seminaries trained pastors to preach and teach, marry and bury. They prepared young men for solo pastorates where they would be expected to fulfill all the functions of a good clergyman. We call this the clergy-laity model. It was clear who was who.

Today, God is changing the way we do church. He is not, however, introducing a new way. He is moving us closer to the model of the early church—to the way he originally intended his church to function. Frequently, our ideas about church and ministry are incomplete. In fact, while we're on the subject of perspectives, even our view of God needs to be reconsidered.

The biblical God is described in Scripture as creating all things and all people. He is a loving, relational, and intentional God. He is the one who thoughtfully designed you and me to fulfill a meaningful purpose that will ultimately glorify him and edify others. If we will listen to his voice, he will give us his perspective of who he is and of who we are to be.

## Getting Out of the Boat

Peter was a simple, ordinary man, but he listened to the voice of God. He had a fishing business with his brother. One day, while Jesus was speaking, Peter decided to leave everything and go with Jesus. Peter, who had heard himself described by many people as a fisherman, soon heard Jesus describe him as a fisher of men. The voice of Jesus changed Peter's understanding of who he was and what he was to do. He did not fully grasp it all at the time, but as he continued to follow Jesus, he discovered Jesus' purpose for his life.

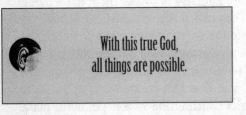

With this true God, all things are possible.

Toward the end of one very busy day, Jesus instructed his followers to get into a boat and sail across the Lake of Galilee. Jesus needed to spend some time alone and would catch up with them later. So off they went. Many of these men were experienced sailors who earned their livelihood from those Galilean waters. That night a tremendous head wind came up causing huge waves to crash against the boat.

In the darkness of the night, Jesus approached the boat, walking on the water. When his followers saw someone coming toward them that way, they were terrified, thinking it was a ghost. Jesus spoke, "Have courage and don't be afraid!"

Peter quickly responded. He asked Jesus to tell him to come to him.

Jesus said, "Come."

Peter got out of the boat and started walking on the water toward Jesus. Then Peter changed his focus. He noticed the wind and waves and started to remember that people don't walk on water. He must have thought, *What am I doing out here?* When his focus shifted from Jesus to the circumstances around him, he became afraid and began to sink. Jesus lifted him up out of the water saying, "You of little faith. Why did you doubt?"

It would be easy to come to the conclusion that Peter simply did not have enough faith. But what about the others who never got out of the boat? Peter had enough faith to walk on water, an experience the others never had.

Peter obeyed the voice of Jesus to come. This obedience resulted in something the fisherman could never have accomplished on his own. As long as he was focused on Jesus, he did just fine, but when Peter's attention turned to his circumstances, he was no longer able to continue walking on the water. Peter's focus was the difference.

## Obeying His Voice, Doing the Impossible

Are you focused on Jesus Christ? Do you hear him saying to you, "Come"? Like Peter, if Jesus calls you to something, you can be sure he will provide the power to accomplish it if you stay focused on him. I believe that Jesus is calling each one of us. His calling is consistent with his design and creation of our unique person. If we will hear him and focus on him, we will accomplish things we would never have thought possible.

But we have to get out of the boat. There is no other way to see and experience the power of God in our lives. Each of us will have our own walking-on-water experience when we obey Jesus— when he says to us, "Come," and we step out with our God-given passion, spiritual gift, and personal style.

Lord,
    Allow me to see things through your eyes.
Teach me what ministry really means.
    Show me what your church is supposed to be like.
Help me see myself from your perspective—
    with a contribution to make,
with a passion to fulfill,
    with enough faith to hear your voice,
to get out of the boat,
    and to follow wherever you lead.
In Jesus' name,
    Amen.

## Chapter Three

# Where Is My Passion?

I was rushing across town from one meeting to another. Traffic was heavy. I was trying to mentally prepare myself for the next meeting. The light was turning red as I moved into the right lane. I was tempted to keep going, but I stopped.

Some movement near the curb caught the corner of my eye. As I turned to see what it was, I noticed a ragged man, about fifty-five years old, digging through the public trash can for a few aluminum cans. He was putting them into his shopping cart with other so-called collectibles.

My thoughts turned from the agenda for my meeting to compassion for the activities of this obviously homeless man. I wondered how he had become homeless. How long had he been on the streets? Did he have a family? A wife? Children? Where were his friends? Did his parents know? Did anybody care? What did he do during the winter nights? When did he bathe? Where did he sleep? Could he work? Why didn't he?

I began to think about other homeless people. Images of homeless children came on my mental screen from the news reports I had seen on TV several nights earlier. I felt saddened and overwhelmed with this social problem. Then the signal turned green, and I was on my way.

I don't do anything for the homeless. Am I a bad person? Some people might say so.

## Pursue Your Heart's Desire

The fact is, I can't care about everything equally. There are some things I care more about than others. That does not diminish the importance of any issue or concern. It simply means that my heart is drawn toward certain involvement. While I have compassion for the homeless, my passion leads me to make other commitments.

Have you ever met someone who believes that youth are the most important age group to reach? He or she will tell you that students are growing and formulating impressions. These students are making the kind of decisions that will influence their own future and the future of those around them. Young people should be told about relationships and the dangers of drugs, alcohol, and sexual promiscuity. "We need to do more for our young people," this person will say, because what he cares most about is serving the needs of youth.

Another individual understands the challenge of working with youth and feels sorry for the homeless. But this individual believes that the Right to Life issue demands everyone's full attention.

Still another person will be committed to evangelism, or overseas projects, or political issues. We could go on and on. There are countless people, functions, and causes that are worthy of our time and best efforts. Since you are not involved in all of them, does that make you a bad person? No. The fact that each of us cares about something more than others is wonderful. Our various passions make it possible for many different people to be involved in meeting many different needs. But what about you?

- What do you care about most?
- For what do you have a passion?
- Where would you like to see your life make a difference?

Sometimes we think of our passion in terms of a *burden* we carry, a *call* we've received, a *dream* we have, or a *vision* we've glimpsed. Whatever you call it, *passion is the God-given desire of the heart to make a difference somewhere.*

If we all cared about the same things, many of the needs in our world would go unmet. But God has put a divine magnet within each of us that is intended to attract us to the people, functions, or causes where he intends us to minister. This is not an afterthought on God's part. Our passion is built in to us so that we will conform ourselves to his purpose for our lives.

Paul was aware that his desire to preach to the Gentiles was not his own agenda but the fulfillment of a desire that God had given him (Galatians 1:15–16). Before entering into a relationship with Christ, Paul had evidenced great zeal for God by persecuting Christians. Then Jesus showed him his blindness, and Paul gained a perspective and understanding of where he was to serve.

There is a relationship between our trusting and delighting in God and the fulfillment of our heart's desire. In order for this relationship to blossom, however, we must understand the purpose the Lord designed for us—a major piece of which is found within our own heart's desire. Yours is

- A heart he uniquely created
- A heart with which he intended to lead you
- A heart meant to draw you to the focus of your ministry
- A heart overflowing with emotional energy—your passion

## Outreach or Obligation?

Edison is remembered for the lightbulb. Ford is remembered for the car. Martin Luther is remembered for the Reformation. For what will you be remembered? Granted, most of us will never be as well known as these people, but fame or huge accomplishment isn't our issue. I'm asking you to consider the matter of personal significance. What do you find most meaningful? Would it be "the family," like James Dobson? Or reaching lost people, like Billy Graham? Or perhaps being merciful, like Mother Teresa? Although your favorite concern may not seem especially significant to someone else, that does not mean it has little value.

Pete and Frank are ushers. Frank gets to the church by 9:15 A.M. every Sunday morning (worship services begin at 10:00 A.M.).

He locates his name tag and places it prominently on his suit coat. He checks the lobby until he locates the bulletins. Several handfuls are strategically placed at the various entrances and on the information table. He quickly goes through the worship center to make sure there are enough pencils, visitor cards, and songbooks. It is about 9:35 when Frank makes his way to the patio just outside the church's front doors. His excitement builds as he sees cars pulling into the lot and people making their way to the building. With a warm smile and sincere greeting, Frank makes sure everyone finds just what they need.

Then there's Pete. It is 9:55 A.M. by the time he gets to the lobby. He decides to stand at the door to the worship center. There he hands a bulletin to those entering while repeating his monologue with a blank expression and monotone voice saying, "Good morning ... Enjoy the service ... Good to see you this morning ... Good morning ..." When the music begins, Pete is relieved to turn his attention toward the service.

Pete and Frank are both ushers. Frank finds it to be a meaningful expression of who he is, but Pete does not. Frank sees the role of usher as a way he can communicate to others that they are important to God, to the church, and to him personally. He has a passion to create a friendly, warm, and nondistracting environment for people to hear and experience the love and grace of God.

Pete, however, does not see ushering as a particularly good use of his time. He feels anyone can do it. In fact, he sometimes wonders why the church doesn't just find a podium and set the bulletins on it so people can pick them up as they come in. He also secretly wishes somebody would install a recorded message on a sound system in the lobby to automatically and repeatedly greet people.

Pete and Frank are examples of two people doing the same task with totally different motivations. Why? One sees ushering as a need in the church that he enjoys meeting. The other sees it as nothing more than an obligation. Is Frank a better person than Pete? Is he more spiritual? Or are they just different?

## Making a Passionate Difference

The difference we're talking about is passion. Do you know what your passion is? If you do not, you are more than likely fulfilling the passions of others. And that is never as satisfying as investing your own God-given passion.

Do those around you express concerns that they find worthy of their time, energy, and resources? Do they communicate these things in such a way that it seems as if something must be wrong with you because you do not feel the same way? The way to respond to other people's concerns is to applaud their passion and pursue your own.

Now we're at the crucial point—what is *your* passion? How would you invest your time, energy, and resources so that at the end of your life you will have a deep sense of fulfillment? How will your life make a contribution to the cause of Christ in the lives of those around you? Perhaps, at the moment, you're not sure. But as you delight yourself in the Lord, you will find the insight you're seeking within the desires of your heart. As you read on, you'll find some help in sorting through the alternatives.

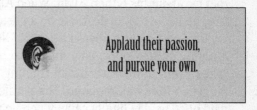

Applaud their passion, and pursue your own.

Perhaps you haven't got a clue what your God-given passion is. Maybe you do know, but you have suppressed it. You may have shared it with a spouse, parent, friend, pastor, or coworker only to have them respond with skepticism or dismay. You may have heard:

- "Why on earth would you want to do that?"
- "You're not smart enough" (or "spiritual enough" or "old enough").
- "But you're a woman!"
- "That would be irresponsible."
- "You don't have the money."
- "That's great, but would your parents (or children or pastor or spouse) approve?"

When that sort of response occurs, there is often a nervous smile, polite agreement, and a painful pushing of passion back into the depths of the heart. Passions are hidden but not gone; silenced but still speaking to us. We may suppress our God-given passion, but it will not go away. Like a beach ball submerged under the surface of the water, it will keep popping up.

How long will you continue spending energy on keeping your passion submerged? A few months, a few years, or an entire lifetime? When you come to the end of your life, will you blame God, your family, or the church for your never having accomplished your life's purpose? What will you say to the Lord as you stand before him on the day of accountability? Will you have to make excuses, or will you hear what we long to hear Jesus say to us, "Well done, good and faithful servant! I'm proud of you"?

## A Passion for a Lifetime

Charlie and I were talking about these things one day, and he told me about his father, Allan. When Allan was in his early twenties, he had a strong desire to be a missionary pilot. The training for that particular career is rigorous. Not only do you have to be a highly skilled pilot, you must also be a master mechanic. It takes years of dedication and training to qualify. Allan had the diligence that was required. His persistence and determination paid off. The day finally came when he received his certification.

Allan then sought out a mission agency and applied for the position that would bring together his two greatest passions— mission work and flying. He was not accepted. To this day he does not know why. For the next twenty years after being rejected, Allan was a janitor at a local high school. It was an honorable job, but his dream was submerged.

Charlie said that even today when Allan is around planes or is involved with mission projects, he is a different person, demonstrating intense energy and enthusiasm. Missions and flying remain his passion.

Years of disappointment, rejection, and suppression did not change Allan's passion. And they will not change yours. Our passion is God-given and meant to be expressed. Submerging it for twenty years will not make it go away, so why not let it surface and come out? Use your energy to discover and fulfill the calling to which you have been called.

Identifying your God-given passion is not an exact science; it is more of a process. Let's first define passion and consider several categories. Then, we will look at seven different ways you might come to realize and identify your passion. Finally, we will explore some reasons why your passion may be hard to identify. Isn't it time you got in touch with this important aspect of yourself?

## Definition and Categories of Passion

We have identified passion as the God-given desire that compels us to make a difference in a particular area of ministry or life where God is glorified and people are edified.

The various passions we find among different people don't have anything to do with who is right or wrong. Passion is not about being good or bad. If our passion is God-given, it is an issue of obedience. Will you be faithful to the passion God has placed in your heart?

There is a danger in putting things into categories, because categories often narrow the possibilities. There is a risk in defining your passion because words are more limiting than are nonverbal expressions. Our hope with the following categories is that the desires of your heart can be identified so you'll better understand your passion for service.

Most of the thousands of people I have worked with through the years would be able to put their passion into one of three general categories. Be aware that there can be some overlap in the way you articulate your passion, and please feel free to use your own words or phrases as you consider your own concerns.

## Passions About People

Passions about people include people groups like children, youth, or senior citizens. People groups can involve those who are grieving, newly married, or blind. You might have a passion for the mothers of preschoolers, for immigrants, or for the unemployed. If you have a *people-passion*, you long to be identified as one who makes a difference in certain people's lives.

## Passions About Roles or Functions

Passions about roles or functions might include things like discipling, being an entrepreneur, or consulting. If you're one of these people, you'll find it most fulfilling to serve in a particular role. It could be in terms of a passion to learn, solve problems, or develop systems.

People who favor roles or functions often list several passions, but careful assessment reveals that they are filling similar roles in each of the areas on their list. Yours might be the role of provider, instructor, or researcher. In your *function-passion*, you long to serve in a specific role, but your passion may find its expression in different arenas.

## Passions for a Cause

People who are cause-driven believe that *their* cause is the significant issue in life that needs to be addressed if God is to be truly glorified and the cause of Christ advanced.

Some have a passion for addressing the problems of world hunger, fighting for human rights, the environment, financial stewardship, or reaching the spiritually lost. If you have a *cause-passion*, you will enthusiastically attempt to make others aware of the issue and attract as many as you can to become supporters.

With cause-oriented passion, you may continuously feel a level of frustration with the fact that more people are not as passionately committed to the cause as you are. They may be sympathetic, occasionally involved, and even give financially, but the bottom line is that they just do not care about it as much as you do. Again, we can't all do everything. Ask yourself: *Am I doing anything about my heart's desire? Am I fulfilling my passion and finding fulfillment?*

## Passion Indicators

There are seven passion indicators that may be helpful in the identification of your passion.

1. Imagine that you and I are meeting for the first time. In the course of our conversation, we talk about a variety of topics. Then we turn to a new subject. As you are talking to me about it, you start speaking a little faster. You lean forward. You become increasingly animated. Your voice goes up a little. Your passion may be indicated by more active body language. You are talking about a subject that could keep you up late at night. It's the topic that would cause you to jump out of bed in the morning. What are we talking about?

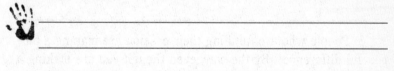

_____

_____

_____

_____

2. Sometimes our dreaming or reflection allows us to imaginatively explore the desire of our heart. In these times, we may visualize or find ourselves being drawn as if by a current toward something that heightens our feelings and enlarges our capacity for action. The image that we see will hit an emotional chord. When you are alone, do you ever wonder, "What if . . .?" Does your response to that question create emotional energy? What is it?

_____

_____

_____

_____

3. Make a list of your greatest achievements, but be sure that they are things you enjoyed doing. These achievements may be accomplishments that others do not find particularly impressive, but are were important to you. (Conversely, you may have achieved Student of the Year, but to you it was not that big of a deal, or you did not enjoy the process of earning it.)

Perhaps when you were twelve, you and a friend decided to put on a neighborhood carnival. You organized the booths, got people to run them, had prizes, made and sold tickets, and actually made a little profit. You pulled it off and had a great time doing it. It was an enjoyable achievement. Are there similarities in your list of enjoyable achievements? What themes can you see?

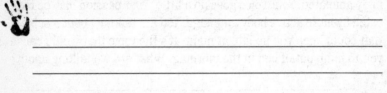

4. What kinds of things are you doing? What topics are you involved in, in which you lose track of time? When you are moving in the direction of your passion, time can easily slip away. Our passion can make us less aware of what is going on around us because we become so focused on what we care about most. What might that be?

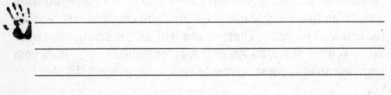

5. People who are fulfilling their passion are making a purposeful difference. (By the way, even though you are making a difference, it doesn't necessarily mean you are serving in the area of your passion.) Those who are expressing their heart's desire will find greater energy and focus as they positively impact those around them.

Of course, the process of fulfilling your passion will not always be easy or fun. But in the midst of moving toward your passion, there is an inner confidence that you are doing what God wants you to do in the way he wants you to do it. There is an assurance that you are where he wants you, and that he is using you according to his divine purposes. Whether subtly or overtly, you are making a difference. Where is that happening? In what area would you like to see it happen?

_____

_____

_____

_____

6. Your passion will energize you. Not only will you become more alive emotionally, but the activity or thoughts about your passion will actually give you energy. This is God's way of moving you toward those people, roles, or causes that are his created agenda for your life. His will for you is partly revealed in your God-given passion. What energizes you?

_____

_____

_____

_____

7. Whatever your passion is, it needs to be submitted to a twofold test: Does it glorify God? Does it edify others? If your passion and its expression do not meet this test, you have not identified your God-given passion. You may have expressed a desire of your heart, but it is not from God. He cannot violate his own integrity and purposes. That is why we are shown the condition on which God will give us the desires of our heart, "Trust in the Lord and do good; dwell in the land and enjoy safe pasture. Delight yourself in the LORD and he will give you the desires of your heart" (Psalm 37:3–4).

Jesus was communicating the same principle in the New Testament when he said, "If you abide in Me, and My words abide in you, ask whatever you wish, and it shall be done for you" (John 15:7 NASB).

Many people are asking God for things, but they are not abiding in Jesus. When we abide, we can confidently ask, knowing that he will be pleased to respond to our requests because they will reflect his purposes. His heart's desire for us becomes our heart's desire. Does your passion glorify God and edify others? When you are abiding and delighting yourself in him, what desires do you have?

_____

_____

_____

_____

Reviewing your responses from above, how might you summarize your passion in a word or phrase?

I have a passion for (to):

_____

_____

_____

_____

## Passion Confusion

You may still be feeling confused about what your real passion is. There are a number of factors that can make it difficult for you to get a handle on your passion. Let's consider a few of them.

### Surrounding Values

Sometimes the values of those around us are so dominant or rigid that our departure from them creates feelings of rejection or a lack of approval. Growing up in a variety of environments such as our home, church, and school, we may have felt differently than those who were in positions of authority. Because we trusted them, we adopted what they valued. For some of us, doing so meant abandoning our own interests.

Our need to belong may have caused us to submerge our own passions for passions more "acceptable" to those around us. If you knew there would be no family or friend to judge your behavior, what would you do?

## Pleaser Personality

It seems that those who have a strong orientation toward pleasing others have a more difficult time identifying their own passion. Whether one's motivation for pleasing is intentional or a result of some subconscious emotions, the result is the same. For people like this, it feels illegal or selfish to say, "I want to ..."

## Unrecognizable Theme

Some people list four, five, or more passions and are not able to narrow it down to one. They cannot seem to find any harmony in their list. These people may require more prayer and reflection to discern the core of their passion. Sometimes we are not able to see the central theme of our passion because of the various ways we are expressing it. A trusted friend can be helpful in talking through our interests in order for us to be able to find a word or brief phrase that captures the essence of our passion.

## Terminology

The term *passion* may be a mental block to the understanding of desire for ministry. If you have used words like *vision*, *dream*, *burden*, or *call* in the past to describe your special desires, the word *passion* might create a different way of thinking about God's intended purpose for your life. By viewing your passion in the same way as you view these other terms, you may be able to think more concretely about your passion's connection to purposeful action.

### The Where Question

As you identify and pursue your God-given passion, you will become more aware of the answer to the question we have been asking, "Where should I serve?" Naming your passion answers the *where* question.

- If you have a passion for children, where should you be serving?

  *In a ministry that is committed to impacting the lives of children.*

- If your passion is for discipleship, where should you be serving?

  *In a ministry committed to discipling people.*

- If your passion is for world hunger, where should you be serving?

  *In a ministry or organization committed to feeding the poor.*

- My passion is _____ , so where should I be serving?

  *In a ministry committed to _____ .*

Don't worry at this time how you can fulfill your passion. Don't let the fact that your church may not have such a ministry keep you from identifying your passion. For now, we just want you to name it.

God has indicated where he wants you to serve—it has been written on your heart. But knowing where to serve is different from knowing what to do. Your passion may reveal the direction or focus of your ministry, but how do you know what to do within that area of ministry? Fortunately, God has spoken to us about that too.

Lord,
Thank you for placing
your desires in my heart.
Sometimes I have trouble focusing on the things
that matter most to me.
Sometimes I'm confused by the people around me,
and I mistake their passion for mine.
Sometimes I long to fulfill my passion,
but I don't know where you want me to do it.
Please be close to me now.
Help me to stop and be quiet.
Help me to listen to my own heart.
Help me to listen to your still small voice,
and to obey.
In Jesus' name,
Amen.

## Chapter Four

# What's the Big Deal About Spiritual Gifts?

Do you remember the hula hoop? How about bell-bottom pants? Did you ever own a pet rock? Soap-on-a-rope? You may remember them from personal experience, from movies, or from stories you have heard. These sweeping fads created a lot of excitement in their day, yet they seemed to disappear as quickly as they came.

A fad is a temporary focus on a briefly popular fashion. Before long, something new takes its place. A trend, however, is different. Trends are general movements that create lasting changes. They establish new, sustainable, and different directions. Trends are far more established than are fads, regardless of how long they last.

New trends in travel and commuting emerged with the development of the automobile and the availability of roads. Improved farming equipment created the trend of rural migration to cities, as fewer people were needed to farm more acres with greater productivity. The computer has created a trend toward more home offices. What are some trends that you see that are beginning to affect the way you live, work, and relate with others? Cellular phones? Interactive television? The Internet?

Trends affect us all, although they usually emerge slowly and are not easily recognized by the casual observer. They indicate significant patterns and movements that, if properly understood, can help us take advantage of new opportunities and anticipate future needs. Trends flow with the times. They indicate what lies ahead based on what is already occurring. As life moves from one generation to the next, changes that trends bring into our lives are unavoidable.

Over the course of your life, you'll see fads come and go, and you'll gain additional perspectives on how trends impact life. Both fads and trends have caused many people to respond to change differently, with some actively resisting any type of change. Others develop a kind of passive resistance to change. Whether we actively or passively resist, many of us look upon change with some suspicion. This is not only true of the world we live in, but it is also true for the church we gather in.

## Spiritual Gifts: Fad or Trend?

The longer you are a part of the church, the more ministries and programs you will see come and go. It's easy to ignore a new theme, emphasis, or ministry in the church as the latest "spiritual fad." After all, you've seen this kind of thing before—here today, gone tomorrow. Your advice might be to "stay the course," or "just keep doing what we have always done."

Is the present emphasis on spiritual gifts a Christian fad, or is it a new trend in the modern church? Maybe the emphasis on individual contributions involving spiritual gifts is simply a reflection of a dissatisfied "me generation," and the church should not cater to such egocentric needs. How should we understand the recent focus on spiritual gifts that exists in so many churches?

What is taking place in the church today is not a fad. It is not even a trend. It is much more significant than either one, and its impact will be dramatic and far-reaching. The changes being introduced in the church through the identification and expression of spiritual gifts are not a shift toward something new, but a return to the original.

The establishment of the original church in Acts 2 was accomplished by the coming of the Holy Spirit and his ministry within the body of Christ through spiritual gifts that were distributed to each of its members. Centuries later, there was so much confusion and distortion of the truth that it took the Reformation to redirect believers back to God's original design. While many changes have taken place in the church as a result of that Reformation, those changes were not attempts to do something new, but rather to return to the biblical model, to the way God intended us to be as the church.

The Reformation reestablished the centrality and authority of the Bible, with faith, accomplished through the power and grace of Jesus Christ alone, being the means for receiving forgiveness of sin. While the Reformers talked about the priesthood of all believers and the equipping of the saints, those practices were rarely incorporated into the way the church functioned. Men like Martin Luther understood the importance of putting the ministry back into the hands of the people (laity), but the leadership (clergy) of their day were not able to bring that concept into reality.

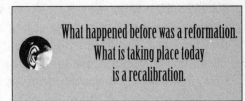

What happened before was a reformation. What is taking place today is a recalibration.

Today, right before our eyes, God is placing ministry back into the hands of every believer across denominational and geographical boundaries. And he is doing it through a movement of his Holy Spirit. We are in the midst of a new reformation. The first Reformation *was*, and today's reformation *is* God's action in bringing the church back to being a biblical community with integrity (Acts 2:42–44). By functioning in greater accord with spiritual gifts (1 Corinthians 12), the church is more able to fulfill the great commission (Matthew 28) for greater ministry to the world. And he'll keep working with us until we've completed the work that he has in mind (Philippians 1:6).

## Spiritual Recalibration

Have you ever had a wind-up toy car? After several good twists of the crank, you set it on the floor, aim it in the right direction, and let it go. While I assume that these toys were designed to go straight, most of the wind-up cars I've had have curved off to the right or the left. After a number of unsuccessful launches, I usually ended up modifying the car's aim from the start so it would end up where I wanted it to go.

Here's another example: Have you weighed yourself lately? Were you at all surprised by the result? Did you wonder if the scale was accurate? We all know that while scales are supposed to be true indicators of our weight, they often get out of adjustment.

What would you do if you thought the scale was not accurate? You would get off and see if it was pointing at zero. If you discovered it was pointing at eight, you would find the adjustment knob and reset it at zero. Most scales are set by the factory, but they have been designed with the ability to be reset.

In the same sense, the growing awareness and use of spiritual gifts today are divine adjustments for a church made by God and built with the ability to reset itself. God wants his original plan for the church to be rediscovered, and he has set the process in motion through the power of the Holy Spirit. This movement is not a fad; it will not go away. And it is more than a trend taking us to something totally new. Today's focus on the gifts is a spiritual recalibration.

## Perspectives on Spiritual Gifts

Of course, change doesn't come easily. The subject of spiritual gifts elicits a variety of responses among Christians, ranging from absolute ignorance of the subject to disinterested feelings of, "Oh, I already know all about that!" Along the emotional spectrum, Christians respond to talk about spiritual gifts with either warmth and blessing or with pain and discord.

Another continuum is the theological spectrum that says, on one end, that some of the spiritual gifts such as tongues, healing, or miracles don't exist today. On the other end, we are told that all the gifts are active and ought to be expressed. There are also various perspectives regarding the number of gifts: Does each believer have only one spiritual gift, or several?

Just looking at this brief summary can raise confusion about spiritual gifts, and it is this confusion that has caused many Christians to avoid the subject altogether. While it is not the purpose of this book to articulate and evaluate the merits of each of these positions, I would like to identify certain biblical directives and expectations for our use of spiritual gifts. Whatever your position experientially, emotionally, or theologically, I trust you will choose to honor God's intention for the personal use of your spiritual gifts in the church.

The fact is, these gifts are vitally important. Before we go on to your particular spiritual gifts, let's look at several reasons why this subject needs to be properly understood. Understanding spiritual gifts will be a blessing to you personally, to the church corporately, and to the world generally.

## Why Do We Need to Know About Spiritual Gifts?

There are a number of reasons why we need to be informed about spiritual gifts.

First, we are told to be aware of them. A pretty simple and clear statement made in 1 Corinthians 12:1 actually amounts to a biblical command: "Now about spiritual gifts, brothers, I do not want you to be ignorant." Ignorance is no excuse. Paul, the writer, is saying, "Listen up! Take note!" The emphasis on gifts is dramatic and critical to a proper understanding of the church and our role within it.

Second, we are expected to use them. As a spiritual father to young Timothy, Paul writes, "Do not neglect the spiritual gift within you" (1 Timothy 4:14 NASB). Would he make such a statement if neglect were not a possibility? Unfortunately, such neglect happens every day. There are believers who have been given a spiritual gift and are not using it for its intended purposes. In some cases, they are ignorant. For other believers, disobedience keeps their spiritual gifts from being used in the ministries for which they were created.

The New Testament describes the church as a body. A leg that does not get any exercise will, over time, atrophy and look deformed. The rest of the body then has to compensate and carry the "dead weight." This compensation looks unnatural, and it is clearly not the way the body was originally designed to function.

In the same way, some members of the body of Christ are not exercising their spiritual gifts. This means that the rest of the body must work extra hard to make up for their lack of contribution. Men and women with too many duties get stressed, overcommitted, and burned out. What if every believer was using his or her spiritual gifts? There would be greater joy, appropriate commitments, and energized service. The body of Christ would properly function and be a healthy place for worship, ministry, and reaching a lost world.

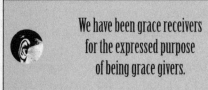

We have been grace receivers for the expressed purpose of being grace givers.

Third, we are stewards and will be held accountable for the use of our gifts. Peter, another leader in the early church, writes to all those who will listen, "As each one has received a spiritual gift, employ it in serving one another as good stewards of the manifold grace of God" (1 Peter 4:10 NASB).

Spiritual gifts are literally "grace gifts." A portion of the grace we have received from God has come in the form of these gifts and we are to wisely manage, or be stewards of, these graces.

The Creator knows our need to be needed. He designed us with a longing to belong. In meeting the needs of others, we find the satisfaction of being connected with them. Our sense of belonging is validated by the mutual ministry of grace givers (those able to meet a need) and grace receivers (those able to have a need met).

Our divine endowments, or spiritual gifts, are not given for us to keep them to ourselves. They are ours to use as we further the kingdom in the world today. There is no better illustration of this than the story Jesus told in Matthew 25:14–30 of a generous boss who left for an extended trip. He gave three of his employees some money to use while he was gone. One received ten thousand dollars, another five thousand dollars, and the other, one thousand dollars.

When the boss returned, he summoned the three and inquired as to how they had done. The first brought twenty thousand dollars, saying he'd managed an investment portfolio and was able to double its net worth. The boss was pleased at how well he had done and told the employee how proud he was of him.

The second employee had much the same story to tell. He laid his original five thousand on the table plus five thousand more that he had netted in a number of land transactions. The boss's pleasure was reflected on his face as well as with words of praise and appreciation. He too had done well.

By this time, the third employee was feeling a little embarrassed. There was a mixture of fear and pride in his voice as he explained how he had taken the one thousand and had stuck it in a safe place. With a slight smile and a little apprehension, he told the boss that he had hidden the money where no one would find it. Then he handed the boss the same one thousand dollars.

There was an uncomfortable moment of silence that seemed to last for hours. The boss was visibly surprised and disappointed. Looking deeply into the employee's eyes, he appropriately expressed his frustration at the man's irresponsible actions.

In his defense, the employee said that he thought the boss would have been upset if he'd lost his money. That being true, the boss was stunned that the employee hadn't at least put the money in the bank to draw simple interest. The employee was fired for not being able to manage and be a proper steward of important resources.

This version of a story that Jesus told long ago emphasizes the point that God expects a return on his investment. Someday we will give an account for the resources he has given us to manage. We are to be stewards of our spiritual gifts in a way that glorifies him and edifies others.

How are you doing as God's steward? Are you aware of what you have been given? Are you keeping your gifts stuck away in a safe place, or are you investing them for the kingdom?

## Definition of a Spiritual Gift

God has been very clear about the reasons for knowing and using our spiritual gifts. But what exactly is a spiritual gift? We will use the following definition: *Spiritual gifts are divine abilities distributed by the Holy Spirit to every believer according to God's design and grace for the common good of the body of Christ.*

Let's take a closer look:

*Spiritual gifts are divine abilities . . .* They are endowments or special skills given by God that enable us to make our unique contribution. They are not natural talents, but divine abilities that enable us to do ministry.

*. . . distributed by the Holy Spirit . . .* These divine abilities created by God are given to believers when they become members of the body of Christ through the Holy Spirit. Not only does the Holy Spirit distribute the gifts, he empowers us in our use of them for meaningful ministry contributions (1 Corinthians 12:7, 11, 18).

*. . . to every believer according to God's design and grace . . .* There is no Christian without a spiritual gift. Every believer has at least one. Gifts equip believers to fulfill the Lord's purpose by reflecting his design for their lives.

*. . . for the common good of the body of Christ.* Your spiritual gift is not for you, but given to you for others. The divine ability you have been given enables you to meet a need in other individuals and the church as a whole. Each of us can make a kingdom difference. Our gifts allow us to serve one another better. They enable us to glorify God and to edify others (1 Corinthians 12:7).

## The Benefits of Spiritual Gifts

When your spiritual gifts are used, there are personal, church, and kingdom benefits. Let's look at some of them.

### Personal Benefits

*Once you know and use your spiritual gifts, you will know your spiritual job description.* Are you committed to doing God's will for your life? Then you will surely do a careful assessment in identifying your spiritual gifts. He has given you the spiritual gifts necessary to do his will. By knowing your gifts and using them accordingly, you will be better able to accomplish his purposes for your life. Your gifts will help show you what to do:

> If God has given you the spiritual gift of encouragement, he wants you to encourage.
>
> If God has given you the spiritual gift of teaching, he wants you to teach.
>
> If God has given you the spiritual gift of helps, he wants you to help.

*When you know your spiritual job description, your ministry will be more focused.* Otherwise, it is easy to get involved with other activities to the neglect of your specific area of contribution. Your spiritual gift defines your best expression.

> Therefore, I urge you, brothers, in view of God's mercy, to offer your bodies as living sacrifices, holy and pleasing to God—this is your spiritual act of worship. Do not conform any longer to the pattern of this world, but be transformed by the renewing of your mind. Then you will be able to test and approve what God's will is—his good, pleasing and perfect will. (Romans 12:1–2)

We are able to present our bodies as a living sacrifice by identifying and expressing our spiritual gifts (Romans 12:3–8). Ministry through the gifts of the Spirit is the active presentation of oneself, which in turn is spiritual worship. Serving through our giftedness is a pleasing form of worship. It not only reveals God's purpose for us personally but also identifies our role within the church community.

In addition to knowing your spiritual job description, *your ministry will be more fruitful and fulfilling when you know and use your spiritual gifts.* Jesus said, "This is to my Father's glory, that you bear much fruit, showing yourselves to be my disciples" (John 15:8). It is God's intention that we bear fruit. If we don't, it is not God's fault. Our divine ability (or spiritual gift) makes it possible for us to get the kind of results that will not only glorify God, but will edify others.

A few verses later, Jesus says, "These things I have spoken to you, that My joy may be in you, and that your joy may be made full" (John 15:11 NASB). Not only does Jesus expect us to be fruitful, he anticipates that we will be full of joy. When we are serving with our spiritual gifts, we are more likely to be both fruitful and fulfilled. Our ministry experiences will be personally satisfying because there is an assurance that we are making a kingdom difference and giving pleasure to God.

## Church Benefits

*There is more unity and harmony in churches that teach and develop gift-based ministries.* Confusion and disharmony exist in churches where there is a lack of appreciation for the unique contributions of individuals. We often observe the differences in others as obstacles. But God views them as opportunities to serve one another in a variety of ways, meeting diverse needs in the church and in the world.

Have you ever been to a meeting where one person is deeply concerned about who is to do what by when? Someone else seems to be preoccupied with looking out for the most needy person in the group. Another person at the meeting doesn't say much and appears to be a little bored, wishing someone would tell her what to do.

One of these people has a spiritual gift of administration, another has a mercy gift, and the other has a gift of helps. When you understand this, you will hear their concerns and receive their comments with greater understanding and gratitude.

Jesus, the head of the church (Ephesians 1:22; 4:15–16), has designed each of us, members of his body, to function in ways that complement and meet the various needs within the body. Knowing and using our spiritual gifts will clarify God's purposes and give direction for our ministry together. It will make us less inclined to see our differences as obstacles. We will be more enthusiastic about using our spiritual gifts as divine opportunities to glorify God and edify others.

Not only will churches have more harmony, *there is less pride and false humility in churches with gift-based ministries.* When we do not understand spiritual gifts, we are much more likely to take personal credit for our ministry accomplishments. There can be a tendency toward spiritual pride-manifesting behavior that is coupled with phrases like

- "I did ..."
- "Did you see what I .. ?"
- "I'm going to ..."
- "I'm telling you, I ..."
- "I ... I ... I ..."

At the other end of the spectrum are those who practice a kind of false humility. They like to say that the pastor has a spiritual gift, members of the choir have spiritual gifts, and the adult Sunday school teacher has a spiritual gift, but that they themselves, unfortunately, do not. When believers cannot see how to make a significant contribution, they sometimes try to find comfort in the notion that maybe they have no spiritual gift.

These kinds of people take the position of a humble servant who is unable to do any good thing. They say, "I cannot sing like Sandy, I am not an actor like Dan, and I cannot teach like Ted. So I just help out where I can." Although they may sound as if they are being humble, this is false humility. God has said that each of us have received a spiritual gift and we are to use it (1 Peter 4:10).

Both pride and false humility are the result of ignorance. By examining Scripture and personally applying our gifts in the church, we dramatically lower our level of spiritual pride because we will have gained true and appropriate understanding of God's power and his purpose for us. For those who have false humility, sound teaching raises their ownership and responsibility for ministry. They may not know about gifts, or what theirs may be, but as they become informed, they will move from disinterested observers to active participants. When this happens, the whole church benefits.

Finally, *there is maturity and growth in churches that teach and develop gift-based ministries.* It is through the proper functioning of spiritual gifts that the body of Christ grows healthy and strong.

When there are parts of the body of Christ that do not function, or do not function properly, the church body fails to mature and develop as it was intended.

Again, consider the human body. As infants, we depend on livers, lungs, hearts, kidneys, and other organs to function properly for normal growth. When each part makes its appropriate contribution, the body gets stronger, it matures and is able to fulfill its responsibilities. If one, two, or more parts of the body fail to operate, the body is unable to hear, walk, or maybe even breathe.

It is the same for the church, the body of Christ: "Now you are the body of Christ, and each one of you is a part of it" (1 Corinthians 12:27). As one, two, or more of us fail to make our contribution, the church cannot function as intended. Do you ever feel like your church is limping? The first question to ask is, "Am I making my own appropriate contribution?" Have you identified your spiritual gifts? Are you using them? The best place to start is with yourself.

## Kingdom Benefit

*God is glorified and people are edified in the church that teaches and develops gift-based ministries.* God is honored and pleased when the gifts he has given are used to glorify him in ministering to others. Jesus called attention to the kind of deeds that are done in such a way that people may see them and glorify the Father in heaven (Matthew 5:16). When spiritual gifts are properly expressed, people can see the servant's motivation to serve others, noting that these acts of servanthood could only be the result of a heart that has been truly transformed by a loving, gracious, and caring God. This truly models God's love for the world.

We are to love God and love people. It is the essence of our entire relationship with God and one another as evidenced in the Ten Commandments (Exodus 20:1–17) and the Great Commandment (Matthew 22:37–40). Spiritual gifts are for the common good, and as we use them, everything is to be done for the edification of the church. Spiritual gifts give us purpose as the Holy Spirit gives us power to glorify God and edify others.

God has a purpose for your spiritual gift. Do you know what your gift is? How can you really know? These are wise questions to ask, and they will be addressed in the next chapter, "What Are My Spiritual Gifts?" Meanwhile, let's ask God for help with this very important concern.

Lord,
  Thank you for so generously giving spiritual gifts
to every one who belongs to you
    through Christ Jesus.
Help me to better understand
    what those gifts mean to me,
and how I can use my gifts the way you want me to.
    Help me please you by being a good steward.
Help me bless those I love.
    Help me be an active participant in the church.
Enlighten me, Lord,
    and reveal the gift or gifts you have given to me,
so I can use them to bless others and glorify you.
    In Jesus' name,
Amen.

## Chapter Five

# What Are My Spiritual Gifts?

I t wasn't too long after creation that the animals got together to form a school. They wanted the best school possible—one that offered their students a well-rounded curriculum of swimming, running, climbing, and flying. In order to graduate, all the animals had to take all the courses.

The duck was excellent at swimming. In fact, he was better than his instructor. But he was only making passing grades at climbing and was getting a very poor grade in running. The duck was so slow in running that he had to stay after school every day to practice. Even with that, there was little improvement. His webbed feet got badly worn from running, and with such worn feet, he was then only able to get an average grade in swimming. Average was quite acceptable to everyone else, so no one worried much about it—except the duck.

The rabbit was at the top of her class in running. But after a while, she developed a twitch in her leg from all the time she spent in the water trying to improve her swimming.

The squirrel was a peak performer in climbing but was constantly frustrated in flying class. His body became so bruised from all the hard landings that he did not do too well in climbing and ended up being pretty poor in running.

The eagle was a continual problem student. She was severely disciplined for being a nonconformist. For example, in climbing class, she would always beat everyone else to the top of the tree but insisted on using her own way to get there.

Each of the animals had a particular area of expertise. When they did what they were designed to do, they excelled. When they tried to operate outside their area of expertise, they were not nearly as effective. Can ducks run? Sure they can. Is that what they do best? Definitely not.

## People Who Excel

Just as each of those animals has an area in which he or she excels, so do God's people. As a believer, each of us has become "a new creature in Christ" (2 Corinthians 5:17). Part of that new creation is the distribution of what the Bible calls spiritual gifts (1 Corinthians 12). Those gifts enable us to excel, but we will not accomplish much of anything if we aren't doing the things we were intended to do.

We already know that every Christian has been given a spiritual gift. It also bears repeating that spiritual gifts answer the *What should I do?* question. Your gift indicates the role, function, or particular way in which God has intended you to serve. Do you know what the various spiritual gifts are? Do you know *your* spiritual gift?

Many studies have been done and many books have been written on the subject of spiritual gifts. While there is general agreement, most of them vary in their listing of the gifts and the specific descriptions that they give each gift. There is full agreement, however, that God has given spiritual gifts to his followers, and they are to be used to glorify God and edify others.

## What Are the Spiritual Gifts?

There are several passages that mention some of the spiritual gifts (1 Corinthians 12; Romans 12; Ephesians 4; 1 Peter 4). Our list is drawn from these and other passages in order to identify the variety of ways that God has designed the church to serve him, itself, and the world.

As you read about the gifts, reflect on your own ministry and experience. See which of these seem to be most true of you. Also, note which gifts sound like someone you know. Remember, there is no right or wrong spiritual gift. They are just different.

| SPIRITUAL GIFTS | DESCRIPTIONS |
|---|---|
| Administration | The divine enablement to understand what makes an organization function, and the special ability to plan and execute procedures that accomplish the goals of the ministry. |
| Apostleship | The divine ability to start and oversee the development of new churches or ministry structures. |
| Craftsmanship | The divine enablement to creatively design and/or construct items to be used for ministry. |
| Creative communication | The divine enablement to communicate God's truth through a variety of art forms. |
| Discernment | The divine enablement to distinguish between truth and error, to discern the spirits, differentiating between good and evil, right and wrong. |
| Encouragement | The divine enablement to present truth so as to strengthen, comfort, or urge to action those who are discouraged or wavering in their faith. |
| Evangelism | The divine enablement to effectively communicate the Gospel to unbelievers so they respond in faith and move toward discipleship. |
| Faith | The divine enablement to act on God's promises with confidence and unwavering belief in his ability to fulfill his purposes. |
| Giving | The divine enablement to contribute money and resources to the work of the Lord with cheerfulness and liberality. |
| Healing | The divine enablement to be God's means for restoring people to wholeness. |
| Helps | The divine enablement to attach spiritual value to the accomplishment of practical and necessary tasks that free up, support, and meet the needs of others. |
| Hospitality | The divine enablement to care for people by providing fellowship, food, and shelter. |
| Intercession | The divine enablement to consistently pray on behalf of and for others; thus seeing frequent and specific results. |
| Interpretation | The divine enablement to make known to the body of Christ the message of one who is speaking in tongues. |
| Knowledge | The divine enablement to bring truth to the body through a revelation or biblical insight. |
| Leadership | The divine enablement to cast vision, motivate, and direct people to harmoniously accomplish the purposes of God. |
| Mercy | The divine enablement to cheerfully and practically help those who are suffering or are in need. |
| Miracles | The divine enablement to authenticate the ministry and message of God through supernatural interventions that glorify him. |
| Prophecy | The divine enablement to reveal truth and proclaim it in a timely and relevant manner for understanding, correction, repentance, or edification. |
| Shepherding | The divine enablement to nurture, care for, and guide people toward ongoing spiritual maturity and becoming like Christ. |
| Teaching | The divine enablement to understand, clearly explain, and apply the Word of God, thus causing greater Christlikeness in the lives of listeners. |
| Tongues | The divine enablement to speak, worship, or pray in a language unknown to the speaker. |
| Wisdom | The divine enablement to apply spiritual truth effectively to meet a need in a specific situation. |

Isn't it amazing how many different ways we can glorify God and edify others? You may have identified with several of these gifts. Which of the gifts mentioned above seem to be most descriptive of you?

1. _____

2. _____

3. _____

## Confusion About Spiritual Gifts

We have identified many of the gifts mentioned in Scripture and have focused on the reasons, benefits, definition, and descriptions of the spiritual gifts. While we have been focusing on what the spiritual gifts are, we need to be careful not to confuse spiritual gifts with other terms and important concepts.

### Don't confuse spiritual gifts with natural talents.

Talents can be an indicator to your giftedness but do not necessarily equate to your spiritual gift. Everyone has some natural abilities, but God has reserved his spiritual gifts for believers. Only those who have personally trusted Jesus Christ and received his Holy Spirit have a spiritual gift. Let's compare and contrast natural talents and spiritual gifts.

*Natural talents are given at our physical birth; spiritual gifts are given at our spiritual birth.* In the same way that we have particular talents that distinguish us from others when we are physically born, we receive a spiritual gift that enables us to make a unique contribution when we are spiritually born.

Natural talents are an expression of God's common grace to all who have life. Spiritual gifts are his specific grace given to those who have received new life. Although natural talents and spiritual gifts are not the same, *all* that we have ought to and can be used to glorify God and edify others.

*Natural talents may be transformed by the Holy Spirit and empowered as spiritual gifts.* There does not appear to be a definable pattern when a person's natural talents are affirmed as spiritual gifts, but that can be the case for some. For example, some-one may be an effective nurse in the city and be recognized as having a mercy gift in the church. A graphic designer in the work-place may discover that he or she has a spiritual gift of creative communication. And the successful salesperson could be affirmed with the gift of evangelism.

After personally leading over twelve thousand people through this discovery process, I have not been able to identify when, and for whom, a natural talent will be equivalent to a spiritual gift.

In fact, many times there is no correlation between natural talents and spiritual gifts. Being a teacher in the public school system does not mean a person has a spiritual gift of teaching. Being an effective manager in the marketplace does not guaran-tee anointed leadership or administration gifts in the church. In order to determine whether or not there is a relationship between a natural talent and a spiritual gift, ask yourself, *Does my natural ability regularly glorify God and edify others in the church?*

*Both natural talents and spiritual gifts can vary in degree and kind.* Just as there are athletes with tremendous natural abilities and others with less, so too do spiritual gifts fulfill different capacities according to God's purposes.

Just as there are good singers and great singers, some of those with the spiritual gift of leadership will lead tens, others hundreds, and others thousands. Some with the gift of helps will use their gift in specific ways each time, while others with the same gift will help in a variety of ways and situations.

*Both natural talents and spiritual gifts are God-given.* Both nat-ural talents and spiritual gifts need to be identified, developed, and used to the glory of God. We are stewards, responsible for all that he has given us. Our talents and gifts are specific ways in which God has extended his grace to us in order for us to be a gracious blessing to others. Your spiritual gifts are your primary ministry contribution to the body of Christ. Your talents may or may not be a contributing factor. We will discuss more about the practical relationship of natural talents and spiritual gifts when we put the pieces together later on.

The chart below summarizes the relationship between natural talents and spiritual gifts.

| NATURAL TALENTS | SPIRITUAL GIFTS |
| --- | --- |
| Given at physical birth | Given at spiritual birth |
| Sometimes a talent can be transformed | Sometimes talents are Holy Spirit empowered |
| • Manager<br>• Salesperson<br>• Singer<br>• Carpenter | • Leadership/Administration<br>• Evangelism<br>• Creative Communication<br>• Craftsmanship |
| Vary in degree and kind | Vary in degree and kind |
| • Athlete<br>• Manager<br>• Musician<br>• Carpenter | • Administration<br>• Leadership<br>• Creative communication<br>• Craftsmanship |
| God-given | God-given |

## Don't confuse spiritual gifts with the fruit of the Spirit.

Both spiritual gifts and the fruit of the Spirit are necessary for us to be productive and fulfilled in our ministry, but they make very distinct contributions.

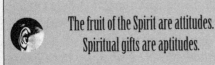

The fruit of the Spirit are attitudes. Spiritual gifts are aptitudes.

*The fruit of the Spirit are "being" qualities; spiritual gifts are "doing" qualities.* "The fruit of the Spirit is love, joy, peace, patience, kindness, goodness, faithfulness, gentleness and self-control" (Galatians 5:22–23). These are inward characteristics of the believer's heart, revealed in their purity and holiness as that person grows and manifests grace. The fruit of the Spirit indicates *what we should be.*

Spiritual gifts are task-oriented functions or roles that God has called and equipped each believer to perform. Spiritual gifts indicate *what we do.* The fruit of the Spirit are attitudes. Spiritual gifts are aptitudes.

*The fruit of the Spirit is a natural by-product of an abiding and obedient relationship with Jesus Christ.* Spiritual gifts are given when we become Christians, and they are always a part of us. Obedience and submission to Christ will, over time, transform our selfish and sinful hearts to produce yielded hearts that evidence authentic fruit such as love, joy, peace, and all the others.

*Both the fruit of the Spirit and spiritual gifts are essential for effective ministry.* Spiritual gifts and fruit of the Spirit both need to be developed. God is not as much concerned with what we do as he is with the spirit in which we serve. For example, if we use our spiritual gifts to the fullest but do not have love, it does not please God or make a kingdom difference (1 Corinthians 13:1–3).

To maximize our ministry and life potential, we need to express both the fruit and the gifts. What are the gifts without love? What is love without the expression of gifts? Which wing of the airplane is most important? Both are essential for a successful flight.

| FRUIT OF THE SPIRIT | SPIRITUAL GIFTS |
| --- | --- |
| "Being" qualities | "Doing" qualities |
| Attitudes | Aptitudes |
| By-product of healthy walk with God | Supernatural endowment of the Spirit |
| Necessary for effective ministry | Necessary for effective ministry |

## Don't confuse spiritual gifts with spiritual disciplines.

Each of us should be developing habits that keep us spiritually and relationally healthy. These disciplines are activities evidenced in some measure in the life of every fully devoted follower of Jesus Christ.

*Spiritual disciplines strengthen the individual; spiritual gifts strengthen others.* Spiritual disciplines are important habits believers develop in order to be strengthened, so they can walk in the world without being conformed to it. Disciplines essentially put believers in positions of submission to worship the majesty of God, hear the voice of God, see the face of God, feel the touch of God, learn the Word of

God, discern the will of God, receive the power of God, and be nurtured in the love of God, in order to extend the grace of God.

We can be strengthened through such disciplines as prayer, study of the Word, solitude, fasting, journal writing, simplicity of lifestyle, and sacrificial giving, to name a few. The disciplines are significant habits for personal growth. Spiritual gifts, on the other hand, are important contributions that strengthen and enable growth in the body of Christ.

*Spiritual disciplines are habits that enable believers to become fully devoted followers of Jesus Christ.* Spiritual disciplines are some of the many ways we receive grace. Spiritual gifts are the specific ways we extend that grace.

| SPIRITUAL DISCIPLINES | SPIRITUAL GIFTS |
| --- | --- |
| Strengthens personal growth and devotion | Strengthens ministry growth and effectiveness |
| Develops devotion | Expresses devotion |
| Examples: Prayer Study Fasting | Examples: Intercession Knowledge Mercy |

## Don't confuse spiritual gifts with ministry positions.

There can be a relationship between gifts and ministry positions, but there is not necessarily a one-to-one correspondence.

*Ministry titles indicate general roles; spiritual gifts indicate specific functions.* Sometimes individuals in the position of pastor do not have a spiritual gift of shepherding. As they pastor the church, they may be doing so primarily though their spiritual gift of leadership, mercy, or administration.

Many who faithfully serve as small-group leaders do not have a spiritual gift of leadership. They may be using their spiritual gifts of teaching, encouragement, or shepherding to lead the group. All this is perfectly acceptable if we are clear on what the role is and what the person's spiritual gifts are.

*Ministry titles indicate organizational positions; spiritual gifts indicate ministry contributions.* When we confuse gifts with titles, we can create inappropriate expectations of those serving in various positions. Knowing your spiritual gift will indicate how you will most effectively function within whatever organizational position you are in.

| MINISTRY POSITIONS | SPIRITUAL GIFTS |
|---|---|
| General roles | Specific functions |
| "Titles" of positions | "Tasks" to perform |
| Examples: | Examples: |
|    Pastor |    Teaching |
|    Small Group Leader |    Shepherding |
|    Sunday School Teacher |    Prophecy |
|    Mercy Team Member |    Encouragement |

Spiritual gifts cannot be used effectively when there is confusion surrounding what they are and how God intends them to be expressed. Knowing what your spiritual gifts are and how God intended them to function within the church is crucial for you, the church, and the world. It usually takes more than reading about spiritual gifts to identify them. Ongoing prayer, study, experience, and reflection will provide the additional insights you need to avoid confusion and to serve according to your giftedness.

## Your Passion and Spiritual Gifts

By now, we've examined where you should serve and what you should do. Your passion reveals your heart's desire and your spiritual gifts indicate your task abilities. As you can see, these are not the same thing. You will see how they fit together (chapter 7) when your servant profile has been completed.

In the next chapter, we will look at how we relate to others and the world around us. How is it that some of us are dreamers, while others are realists? Why are some people thinkers, and other people are more feeling-oriented? How is it that some of us are wallflowers, and others are the life of the party? God has given each of us our own personal style to complement our passions and gifts. Before we go on, let's ask him to guide us as we continue to learn.

Lord,
    Thank you for the amazing array of gifts
you have poured out upon your people.
    And thank you for giving a special gift to me,
so I can participate in the church
    according to your perfect plan.
Please help me to recognize my gift.
    If I have ignored it, forgive me.
If I have suppressed it, stir it up.
    Direct my thoughts toward
my appropriate area of service,
    And empower me to become everything
you created me to be:
    fruitful, joyful, loving, faithful, and grateful.
In Jesus' name,
    Amen.

## Chapter Six

# How Do I Relate with My Personal Style?

I want you to try something. When I tell you what it is, don't just think about it, actually do it. It's simple: set this book down and cross your arms in front of you. Get comfortable. With your arms crossed, glance down and notice the position of your hands and arms. Okay?

Do it now.

Great! Now I'd like you to do it again. But this time, put the arm that was on top underneath, and put the arm that was underneath on top. In other words, reverse your arms. Got it? Do it.

It wasn't as easy to do that time, was it? Did it feel awkward? Uncomfortable? Did you really have to think about how to do it? I did.

The first time you crossed your arms, it was quite natural, easy, and did not require much thought because you did it the way you always do it. Each of us cross our arms a certain way, and no arm-crossing technique is right or wrong, good or bad. They are just different.

## Personal Preferences

Your God-given personal style is the way you prefer to relate to the world around you. It is the third element in your servant profile, complementing the expressions of your passion and your spiritual gift. Your personal style answers the *How can I best serve?* question.

You have been created with preferences—choices you make when relating to others. You are more comfortable relating in some ways than in others. Certain responses come more naturally to you.

In various situations, you may not feel the freedom to express yourself naturally. No matter where you are—with a spouse, friend, or fellow employee; in a family system, school, church, or small group—you can certainly relate in ways other than your preferred style, but it isn't as comfortable. When relationships don't permit your preferred style, they require additional time, energy, and sensitivity.

What if you could serve God in ways that reflected your personal style? What if you could find ministry opportunities that actually required someone with your style? You can be sure of one thing—you'd experience far more energy for ministry!

## How Are You Energized?

Personal style is sometimes referred to as personality or temperament. It describes your most natural way of relating to others. Your personal style is unique to you, and it energizes you.

There are some kinds of activities that give us energy and some that seem to take energy from us. God has wired us to be energized by certain interactions. They provide us with the energy needed in other situations that are draining. Consider:

- Do you find interactions with people to be energy producing? Or . . .
- Do you get energy from the completion of a task?

Every time Greg has to attend a meeting, he arrives early. He likes to talk to his friends before the meeting actually gets started. It is important for him to catch up with what has taken place in other people's lives since they last met. When he is not able to arrive early enough to mingle with everyone ahead of time, he feels frustrated and unconnected. The details of the agenda do not hold Greg's attention or provide him with enthusiasm in the same way in which being able to touch base with people does.

Sharon comes into the church each Monday morning to sort through the weekend's response cards and prayer requests. She knows where to find them and takes them directly to a computer terminal to input the data. Once it is printed out, she distributes the information to the appropriate ministries. Sharon has an opportunity to visit with some of the staff along the way, but she rarely does. She is energized by being able to get the job done each week so that people's needs can be met.

Being assigned to a cubicle for a weekly task would rob energy from Greg—it would drain his battery. And Sharon wouldn't want to sit around talking with the staff until after she had completed her tasks. Of course, Greg can behave like Sharon, and Sharon can behave like Greg even though they wouldn't really be comfortable. The question is: What gives you energy and what takes your energy?

We function much like a battery—we have to be charged up to be useful. Energy must first be put into the battery so it can be given out. A battery can only give until it is empty. Once it's empty, it is useless, unless it is recharged and made available for use again. Some sources connected to a battery will charge it up; others will drain it.

Are you aware of what energizes you? Do you find people or tasks more fulfilling? Both are needed. Both must be served with excellence. God has created some of us with an orientation to people as our recharging source. Others have been designed to receive energy from the accomplishment of tasks.

This does not mean, if your preference is people, that you do not value the accomplishment of tasks. Nor does it mean that, if your preference is tasks, you do not value relationships. Those two options simply represent your primary and secondary ways of relating to the world around you.

Here's another interesting question: Are you structured or unstructured?

## How Are You Organized?

Terry and Karla are making plans for a vacation together. They will be driving from Chicago to Dallas. Terry wants to pack a bag, throw it into the trunk, and head south. Karla wants to go to the auto club and get all the maps and tour books in order to plan where to stay, which historical markers to see, and what to eat along the way. When free to do so, Terry and Karla organize their lives quite differently: Terry is unstructured. Karla is structured.

Leigh has been asked to speak at a retreat for a group of leaders on the topic, "Reaching Women in Business." Two days before the event, Leigh's secretary asked her how she was planning to approach the subject. Her surprising response was, "I am not sure. I'm taking several speeches with me. I'll wait to get there before I decide which one I will actually use."

It is important for Wayne to have everything in order. He likes to carefully plan his week. And when he knows something has to be done, he would just as soon get it done now and not have to worry about it later. He lines up and prioritizes all of his activities: exercise classes, shopping, work, family time, church, and community involvement. Unstructured Leigh likes options. Structured Wayne likes priorities.

How do you like to be organized? Are you more comfortable when you are able to "play it by ear," "shoot from the hip," "make it up as you go along"? Or do you prefer closure, "just getting it done," "working the plan"?

Most of us can do both. We can behave in a structured or unstructured way, just as we can cross our arms both ways. But one way feels a whole lot more natural. The key question here is, If there were no consequences to the way you organized your relationships and life, would you be a structured or an unstructured person?

## Personal Style Intensity

You have probably been thinking that you are not purely a task- or people-person. You may also have been feeling that you are not quite so unorganized as an unstructured person, but neither are you as comfortable with structure as some very regimented types seem to be.

Personal style is a continuum with the pure 100 percent people-oriented folks on one end and the 100 percent task-oriented folks on the other. You may be more mild or moderate. If you are most energized by mild levels of people interaction, then being put into excessive times of extreme people contacts will give you a similar feeling of disorientation as if you were serving in a moderate to extreme task position. It is the same for the organized continuum.

It is important to recognize your level of intensity because most of us have a zone around us in which we can relate and be fine. But when we consistently operate outside our zone and move further away from our personal-style preferences, boredom or burnout results.

To gain some measure of your style and intensity, work through the following statements. Complete each statement by looking at the word you think best describes what you would naturally prefer to do in most situations. Then circle the number that indicates where you might be on the continuum. For example, if you prefer to be spontaneous while on vacation, then you would circle one or two. Only circle a three if you just don't know what you have a preference for. Total your score for the energized and organized sections.

## How Are You Energized?

1. I'm more comfortable . . .

doing things for people   1   2   3   4   5   being with people

2. When doing a task, I tend to . . .

 focus on the goal   1   2   3   4   5   focus on relationships

3. I get more excited about . . .

 advancing a cause   1   2   3   4   5   creating community

4. I feel I have accomplished something when I've . . .

 gotten a job done   1   2   3   4   5   built a relationship

5. It is more important to start a meeting . . .

on time   1   2   3   4   5   when everyone is there

6. I'm more concerned with . . .

meeting a deadline   1   2   3   4   5   maintaining the team

7. I place a higher value on . . .

action   1   2   3   4   5   communication

*Energized Total E =* _____

## How Are You Organized?

1. While on vacation, I prefer to . . .

be spontaneous   1   2   3   4   5   follow a set plan

2. I prefer to set guidelines that are . . .

general   1   2   3   4   5   specific

3. I prefer to . . .

leave my options open   1   2   3   4   5   settle things now

4. I prefer projects that have . . .

variety   1   2   3   4   5   routine

5. I like to . . .

play it by ear   1   2   3   4   5   stick to a plan

6. I find routine . . .

boring   1   2   3   4   5   restful

7. I accomplish tasks best . . .

by working it out as I go   1   2   3   4   5   by following a plan

*Organized Total O =* _____

If your **E** total was    7–20 you are **energized** through *tasks*.

22–35 you are **energized** through *people*.

If your **O** total was    7–20 you are **organized** by being *unstructured*.

22–35 you are **organized** by *structure*.

The intensity of your personal style is indicated by a score of

| | |
|---|---|
| 7–10 | Concentrated |
| 11–14 | Moderate |
| 15–18 | Mild |
| 19–23 | Undefined |
| 24–27 | Mild |
| 28–31 | Moderate |
| 32–35 | Concentrated |

## Difficulties with Personal Style Identification

Certain people and circumstances may have made it difficult for you to truly understand your personal style. These include your role models (parents, etc.), family and church values (stated or unstated), and dysfunctional or abusive circumstances.

Life is difficult, and many well-meaning (and some not-so-well-meaning) people have shaped our rules about what is appropriate and what is not. We have learned that our acceptance is often conditional upon our willingness to play by the rules. Some required behaviors have not allowed us to relate in ways consistent with our personal style.

Perhaps, while you were growing up, your role models demonstrated different personal style preferences than yours. For example, during your childhood and adolescence, if both your parents were structured and you were unstructured, you might have heard comments like

"You'd better get organized."

"You are such a procrastinator!"

"Why do you always wait to the last minute?"

If both your parents were unstructured and you are structured, you might have heard words like

"You are such a neat freak!"

"I didn't think that assignment was due until next week."

"Just *relax*!"

In order to feel loved and accepted, you may have tried to conform to the style that followed their wishes.

Beyond individual relationships are family systems and church relationships. Within each of these are values that affect the way people interact and how they are perceived. If your personal style conformed to the group, all was probably well. But if your family or church related in a fundamentally different way from the way in which you did, a negative value judgment may have been made against you.

You may have felt devalued because you were not quite like these others. If you continuously chose to behave in so-called acceptable ways, your sense of acceptance and value may have grown, yet you gave up relating with your most natural style and lost something of your intrinsic self.

Abuse can further distort the accurate perception of your God-given personal style. The abuse may be emotional, verbal, physical, or neglectful. The confusion caused by either a one-time event or a sustained pattern of abuse over years is real and can be deeply traumatic. Living with fear will hinder the development of your preferences and your ability to fully receive the love and grace Jesus Christ is forever extending to you. He has made you free—free to be the you he created you to be.

Remember, the God who designed you has not changed. You do not have to continue to live in reaction to the opinions and behavior of others. It's time you became comfortable with the person God made you to be. If it is too painful or confusing to see how you can reach that freedom, see a trusted friend or pastor who may be able either to appropriately help you or to direct you to a professional counselor for assistance.

Sin has made all of us dysfunctional. The more dysfunction we have experienced, the more difficult these matters of identity and purpose can be. When you dare to listen to Jesus say, "Come," and you obey him, you become a proactive force for the kingdom. But as long as you remain confused and inactive, your personal potential is diminished.

Be encouraged. You are in a process. Take what seems to be unclear and seek clarity. Take what you know to be true and turn it into confidence. Experience more of the freedom you have in order to pursue and enjoy your God-given personal style. God's Word will help you find your way.

## Seeing God Through Our Personal Styles

When I became a Christian at the age of eighteen, I had not read the Bible. I was told to start reading the Gospels in order to get to know Jesus better. I read through Matthew and was not too far into Mark's gospel when I realized Mark had copied portions from Matthew! That seemed like plagiarism. As I continued into Luke, I found that he had done the same thing. I was confused. Why did God allow this to happen, especially in the Bible? I began to wonder why there were four gospels. Did God stutter? Why did he need to repeat himself?

Perhaps you have asked the same questions. It wasn't until later that I began to understand his purpose. Each gospel is written to appeal to a different type of personal style. For example, Luke begins with

> Many have undertaken to draw up an account of the things that have been fulfilled among us, just as they were handed down to us by those who from the first were eyewitnesses and servants of the word. Therefore, since I myself have carefully investigated everything from the beginning, it seemed good also to me to write an orderly account for you, most excellent Theophilus, so that you may know the certainty of the things you have been taught. (Luke 1:1–4)

Would you say Luke is more of a feeler or a thinker? Do you think he would appeal more to a structured or an unstructured reader?

Now consider John, who includes the following expressions in his writings:

> The Word became flesh and made his dwelling among us ... full of grace and truth. (John 1:14)

> For God so loved the world that he gave his one and only Son ... For God did not send his Son into the world to condemn the world, but to save the world through him. (John 3:16–17)

> I am the good shepherd. The good shepherd lays down his life for the sheep ... I know my sheep and my sheep know me ... and I lay down my life for the sheep ... but I lay it down of my own accord. (John 10:11–18)

> Jesus wept. (John 11:35)

> I will ask the Father, and he will give you another Counselor to be with you forever—the Spirit of truth ... I will not leave you as orphans; I will come to you. (John 14:15–18)

> We proclaim to you what we have seen and heard, so that you also may have fellowship with us. And our fellowship is with the Father and with his Son, Jesus Christ.... God is light ... If we confess our sins, he is faithful and just and will forgive us our sins and purify us from all unrighteousness ... Let us love one another, for love comes from God. Everyone who loves has been born of God and knows God ... God is love. (1 John)

John reveals more depth of feeling than logic or reason. He wants to comfort us with the presence, love, and grace of God. Can you feel his emotional effort to reassure the reader about Jesus' departure with the promise that Jesus is going to send us a Counselor?

Most of us do our theology through the eyes of our personal style. We read and relate to biblical truth according to our style preferences. If you are energized through people, you will have a tendency to place a higher value and emphasis on themes like love, forgiveness, fellowship, community, and grace.

If you are task-oriented, you may focus on such themes as going and making disciples, praying, and putting on the armor of God. Obeying, committing, and serving are the concepts that energize you.

Structured people pick up on judgment, law, order, preparation, and justice. Unstructured people gravitate to the understanding of walking by faith, God's giving us the words we need at the appointed moment, trust, being filled with the Spirit, and not worrying.

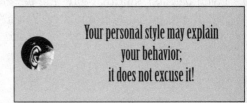

Your personal style may explain your behavior; it does not excuse it!

There are four gospels, so at least one of them will connect with your personal style. No matter how God has wired you, he has provided a means for you to personally relate to him and his Word so that you can best relate to others and the world.

No matter how you see God, you do not see all of him. We need each other to complete the fullness of Christ. We need what we lack in order for the body of Christ to be balanced and healthy. Be the man or woman of God he has made you to be, understanding that what you offer through your personal style is needed but is not complete.

## A Word of Caution

Identifying your personal style will help you to understand why you do some of the things you do in your relationships. That is the good news. (Use care so that it does not become bad news.) The fact is, your human nature is still actively seeking ways to blame others and to creatively rationalize sinful behavior. Keep this important point in mind: Your personal style may explain your behavior; it does not excuse it.

Just because you are unstructured does not mean you can fail to meet deadlines. Being structured does not excuse you of the need to be flexible. Interacting with people will not eliminate the need for completed projects, just as completing tasks does not give you permission to be insensitive, distancing, or abusive.

A significant part of your design is revealed through your personal style. It is another way God has put his divine fingerprint upon you. As a part of your servant profile, your style complements your passion and indicates the unique way your spiritual gift will be expressed.

As we continue, you will see how the integration of your God-given passion, spiritual gift, and personal style provide a meaningful and purposeful ministry. You are on your way to finding what you do best in the body of Christ!

Lord,
 Thank you for the colorful differences
among us all,
 For the way we wonderfully
complement each other.
 Thank you for the people lovers.
Thank you for the task completers.
 Thank you for the careful, precise organizers.
And thank you for those whose lives
 sparkle with serendipity.
Hold up a mirror Lord,
 and show me my true self—
the person you intended me to be.
 Help me to recognize myself,
and to live honestly, fearlessly, and joyfully,
 serving you and your people through the church.
In Jesus' name,
 Amen.

## Chapter Seven

# How Do the Pieces Fit Together?

It was one of those evenings—cold, windy, and rainy. My family and I weren't interested in a board game. There was nothing worth watching on television, so we decided to do a puzzle. Digging through the closet, we found an unopened one at the back of the top shelf. Someone in the family had received it as a Christmas present several years before.

The puzzle had one thousand pieces—clearly it was going to require more time and energy than the six-piece animal puzzle I sometimes put together with my four-year-old son. But it was the perfect activity for just such a night. In fact, as I thought about the challenge we were about to take on, I figured it would capture our best energies for more than one night. We wanted to continue with the puzzle until it was finished, which would probably take a few days. So, out came the card table.

We broke the seal, and once the box was opened, we gathered around while all the pieces were dumped onto the table. Our first task was to get all the colored sides facing up. It wasn't difficult, and it didn't take long, but it was a necessary first step.

Next, we looked for the pieces with straight edges and separated them out. In the process, we were keeping our eyes open for the four corner pieces. They were fairly easy to spot because they were the ones with two straight edges. Not being a master at solving puzzles, I set the top of the box up on the edge of the card table. That way we would know what our finished product should look like.

We took the four corner pieces and started connecting the edges. At that point, I was being guided more by the colors and their placement according to the box than I was by the actual shapes themselves. Once the border was done, it was simply a matter of putting the remaining pieces inside. It ended up being a late night. When we finally went to bed, there were still a lot of pieces on the table that hadn't found their proper places. In fact, it took two more days to complete the puzzle.

Once we had finished, we stepped back and marveled at the many beautiful colors, shapes, and pieces and how they all fit together. When we finally got them where they belonged, the picture was clear and complete.

## Having the Pieces Does Not Guarantee a Picture

Common sense tells us that shaking a box containing all the puzzle pieces and pouring it out on the table will not produce an accurate picture. You can be committed to doing so. You can be persistent. You can take courses on "How to Shake Your Box Creatively." All your efforts and techniques will not get the results you desire. It is not only finding the pieces, but the process of putting them together that leads to a finished puzzle.

The last several chapters have introduced you to the elements of your servant profile. Those elements are important pieces for a picture of your life with God. I imagine that some of the things we've talked about so far have not been totally new to you. They are pieces you've already had, in one form or another, with one level of understanding or another.

Unfortunately, many of us have gone through life and ministry shaking our puzzle box in the hopes that some day we will get the picture. Maybe you're still shaking it. Instead of wasting further time and energy, let's take the pieces of your servant profile and try to form a picture.

## Your Servant Profile

You've already spent some time evaluating your passion, your spiritual gifts, and your personal style. Now, take a moment to review what you've learned. Then summarize it by filling in the information that best describes you.

Name:_____

Passion:_____

Spiritual Gift(s):_____

Personal Style:_____

You have just completed your own servant profile! Are you feeling optimistic and encouraged? I hope you are envisioning some possible new directions for yourself. Can you see yourself serving in ways that reflect who God has made you to be? Does the thought of it inspire you to make a kingdom difference?

## Relationship of Passion to Spiritual Gifts

Before we talk about specific possibilities for service, remember that there is an exciting relationship between your passion and your spiritual gifts. Your passion identifies the desire of your heart to make a difference somewhere. It will help you join others with similar interests. When you gather with those who share your passion, you experience a bond and a common commitment to a particular area of ministry. As your ministry team comes together, each player makes a contribution. Your ministry contribution will be best made through your spiritual gift.

As we've already learned, spiritual gifts are divinely given task abilities. They indicate the way you can best contribute to the fulfillment of your passion. For example, if you had the gift of administration, you would know what to do—administrate. But *where* would you use your gift of administration? That depends on your passion. For example, if your passion is children, you should pursue coordinating and organizing a ministry that is committed to reaching children.

If you are inclined to confuse your passion with your spiritual gifts, it will be helpful for you to phrase your passion in nonspiritual-gift terms. For example, some people state that they have a passion for evangelism. Does that mean they have the spiritual gift of evangelism? Maybe they do; maybe they don't. They might have the gift of prophecy, hospitality, or leadership. It would be better to express that passion in terms of reaching lost people, or reaching the unchurched. Not using spiritual-gift terminology for our passion eliminates potential confusion and frees us to better communicate where we desire to serve versus what we are able to do.

You can combine any passion with any spiritual gift. Don't limit yourself with historical or traditional combinations of the two. Sometimes we have preconceived ideas that aren't really appropriate.

Suppose you told your pastor that with so many new homes being built in the area, you think the church should be trying to reach all those unchurched people. He might assume that you had the spiritual gift of evangelism. But you may not have that gift at all. And if he placed you on a visitation team, you would probably be excited about the opportunity, but you just might not see many people come to Christ.

In a case like this, your desire (passion) to bring people to Christ is being confused with your spiritual gift (encouragement, hospitality, or something else). The two are entirely different, and when we try to make them the same, we confuse two distinct and creative elements of our design.

## Relationship of Spiritual Gifts to Personal Style

Just as there is a relationship between your passion and your spiritual gift, there is also a dynamic between your spiritual gift and your personal style. Any spiritual gift can have any personal style.

We tend to equate some spiritual gifts with certain personality traits. For example, you might confuse the gift of evangelism with an outgoing and somewhat aggressive style. Someone might even say that if you are not able to personally go up to strangers and share the Gospel, you can't possibly have the gift of evangelism. This stereotype has kept many gifted evangelists from using their God-given abilities, because their style is not outgoing and aggressive but more relational and intimate.

Sometimes those with a gift of leadership fail to fulfill their calling because they do not see themselves acting like other leaders. They equate the gift with a specific style. There are many kinds of leaders—according to the measure of faith. There are leaders of tens, hundreds, and thousands. There are visionary leaders and hands-on leaders. Not only is the measure of your gift a factor, but so is the relationship of your personal style.

Let me give two examples: George has a task-structured style. With his gift of mercy, he serves as an advocate for those who need assistance. John's people-unstructured style works best with *his* mercy gift in the role of counselor or friend for those in crisis or pain.

While both men have the same spiritual gift, George serves better on an organizational level, while John serves on the personal or relational level. Both men are needed to minister effectively to those who are in need of mercy.

## Fruitful But Not Fulfilled

Wendy has been involved in her area of ministry for almost two years. She is being fruitful but has not been fulfilled. Wendy's servant profile is

| | |
|---|---|
| Passion: | Help the Homeless |
| Spiritual Gifts: | Encouragement, Mercy |
| Personal Style: | People/Structured |

Wendy's church included four people who shared a passion for the homeless. Since the church was not able to develop and support a ministry to the homeless of its own at that time, they explored a variety of agencies and ministries in the area. After much prayer and interaction with pastoral leadership, the decision was made for the team of four to serve with an existing program in the community.

This placed Wendy on a building crew that constructs or refurbishes homes and apartments that are then made available to the homeless. She has been able to develop some warm relationships with those with whom she serves because they share a common bond. She works alongside Christians and unchurched people alike. Her ministry team from the church meets together before they start working in order to encourage and pray for one another.

Although Wendy has been able to see the fruit of the team's efforts, she has grown increasingly frustrated. She is not experiencing the sense of affirmation or blessing in her ministry that she thought she might. After some reflection and interaction, it became clear why she was not being fulfilled.

Wendy had joined the team because she had an emotional desire (passion) to make a difference with the homeless. She was enthusiastic about what was being done. But she came to realize that her gifts of encouragement and mercy were not being utilized. She was serving with others to help the homeless, but she was never really relating to the homeless people themselves.

Wendy learned that she needed to work firsthand with her gifts and people-orientation. Being a part of the work crew met her passion and her need to be structured, but it did not capture the expression of her gifts. She got energy from interacting with her teammates, but she began to find real fulfillment as she developed personal relationships with the homeless people. Once she put her gifts to work with her passion and her style, Wendy stopped rebuilding homes and started rebuilding lives!

## Possibilities for Your Personal Ministry

Given the elements mentioned above, I'm going to ask you to list some possible positions in which you could express your servant profile. Don't limit your thinking to known positions in your church. Assume there is or could be such a position. What could be the perfect fit for you? What could you do best? Before you begin, let me give you another example: A man named Warren has a servant profile that looks like this:

Passion:          Financial Stewardship
Spiritual Gifts:  Encouragement, Giving, Teaching
Personal Style:   Structured/People

Warren thought of the following possible ministry positions:

- seminar instructor
- budget counselor
- writer of a training process for creating a family budget
- deacon serving on the budget committee
- benevolence board member
- fund-raiser

Based on your servant profile (p. 85), what might be some specific ministry possibilities for you?

1. _____

2. _____

3. _____

4. _____

5. _____

6. _____

7. _____

Go over your list. Did you write down everything you thought of? Don't evaluate how or when you could ever do any of them—we will consider those issues later. For the moment, just identify the possibilities.

It is God's intention that we be both fruitful and fulfilled. Jesus said,

> Remain in me, and I will remain in you. No branch can bear fruit by itself; it must remain in the vine. Neither can you bear fruit unless you remain in me ... If a man remains in me and I in him, he will bear much fruit ... This is my Father's glory, that you bear much fruit, showing yourselves to be my disciples ... I have told you this so that my joy may be in you and that your joy may be complete. (John 15:4–5, 8, 11)

Lord,
    I'm beginning to understand the
reason I enjoy some things about ministry,
    and find others so frustrating.
I am trying to stretch my imagination
    to find the areas of service that best suit
my servant profile.
    But Lord, I need you to lead me to the right people,
to open the right doors,
    to provide me with the right insights and
    opportunities,
so I can be fruitful, fulfilled,
    and at peace in the center of your will.
In Jesus' name,
    Amen.

## Chapter Eight

# What Does God Want from Me?

One day I was driving along a four-lane divided highway when the brake lights of the cars in front of me caught my attention. Traffic slowed. Up ahead, I noticed several police cars stopped on both sides of the road, their red and blue lights flashing. As I drove through this gauntlet of activity, I saw fifteen or twenty men picking up roadside trash, all of them wearing county prison uniforms.

I imagine these men had been jailed for a variety of reasons, but that day they were together, slowly moving along the side of the road with their sticks and orange trash bags. They would poke a piece of trash, look around slowly, then stick it into the plastic bag. After another step or two, each man would poke at something else, slowly pick it up, glance around, and put it in the bag. It was a nice day and they were probably glad to get out. But they were not moving fast or working hard. Their posture and movements reflected futility and a lack of enthusiasm. They were just serving time.

I didn't give the incident another thought until I had a similar experience a few weeks later. I was on another road when brake lights again lit up in front of me. As I slowed, I passed a group of students along the roadside, all with matching T-shirts. This time I recognized them—they were from our church. Our high-school group's annual service project was to work a day in the community, and this team of kids was picking up roadside trash. They were running from one spot to the next, laughing, trying to see who could fill his or her bag first.

What a contrast! The prisoners had demonstrated apathetic indifference, while these students were serving God and others with a contagious enthusiasm. Yet both groups were doing the same task. One group served with energy and joy; the other appeared bored. Which group would you want to be a part of? No question about it, is there? Both were serving, but with two entirely different motivations.

## What Is Your Love Quotient?

We've talked a lot about who we are and what God's purpose for our lives and ministries might be. Now, for a few minutes, let's consider our motivation for doing what we do. What is driving us—really?

The most extensive New Testament passage we have about how the church is to function is found in 1 Corinthians 12–14. We've already drawn a great deal from chapter 12, which provided us with a theological and practical understanding of how the church is to perform as the body of Christ.

Next comes 1 Corinthians 13, the famous "love" chapter. I can't recall attending a church wedding where God's description of love has not been read from it. The depiction of love is true, but the context of the passage is not about marriage. It is about service.

As chapter 12 concludes its teaching on spiritual gifts, chapter 13 begins with the way spiritual gifts are to be expressed. Notice how God's gifts relate to love:

> And now I will show you the most excellent way. If I speak in the *tongues* of men and of angels, but have not love, I am only a resounding gong or a clanging cymbal. If I have the gift of *prophecy* and can fathom all mysteries and all *knowledge*, and if I have a *faith* that can move mountains, but have not love, I am nothing. If I *give* all I possess to the poor and surrender my body to the flames, but have not love, I gain nothing. (1 Corinthians 12:31–13:3, emphasis mine)

Do you see how important love is? You can know your spiritual gift and be using it, but if it is not expressed in love, you will not make a kingdom difference. Consider this love in which we are supposed to serve:

> Love is patient, love is kind. It does not envy, it does not boast, it is not proud. It is not rude, it is not self-seeking, it is not easily angered, it keeps no record of wrongs. Love does not delight in evil but rejoices with the truth. It always protects, always trusts, always hopes, always perseveres. Love never fails.
> (1 Corinthians 13:4–8)

Let's reflect on this key passage a little at a time, breaking it down and applying it very practically to your ministry and your capacity to love. In order to make it more personal, substitute your name in place of *love*. Then rate yourself on a scale from 1 to 5:

1. _____(your name) **is patient.**

   | Seldom | | Sometimes | | Always |
   |---|---|---|---|---|
   | 1 | 2 | 3 | 4 | 5 |

2. _____(your name) **is kind.**

   | Seldom | | Sometimes | | Always |
   |---|---|---|---|---|
   | 1 | 2 | 3 | 4 | 5 |

3. _____ **does not envy.**

   | Seldom | | Sometimes | | Always |
   |---|---|---|---|---|
   | 1 | 2 | 3 | 4 | 5 |

4. _____ **does not boast.**

   | Seldom | | Sometimes | | Always |
   |---|---|---|---|---|
   | 1 | 2 | 3 | 4 | 5 |

5. _____ **is not proud.**

   | Seldom | | Sometimes | | Always |
   |---|---|---|---|---|
   | 1 | 2 | 3 | 4 | 5 |

6. _____ **is not rude.**

   | Seldom | | Sometimes | | Always |
   |---|---|---|---|---|
   | 1 | 2 | 3 | 4 | 5 |

7. _____ is not self-seeking.

       Seldom    Sometimes   Always
       1     2     3     4     5

8. _____ is not easily angered.

       Seldom    Sometimes   Always
       1     2     3     4     5

9. _____ does not keep a record of wrongs.

       Seldom    Sometimes   Always
       1     2     3     4     5

10. _____ does not delight in evil, but rejoices with the truth.

       Seldom    Sometimes   Always
       1     2     3     4     5

11. _____ always protects.

       Seldom    Sometimes   Always
       1     2     3     4     5

12. _____ always trusts.

       Seldom    Sometimes   Always
       1     2     3     4     5

13. _____ always hopes.

       Seldom    Sometimes   Always
       1     2     3     4     5

14. _____ always perseveres.

       Seldom    Sometimes   Always
       1     2     3     4     5

15. _____ never fails.

       Seldom    Sometimes   Always
       1     2     3     4     5

How's your love quotient? Don't be too hard on yourself—perfect love can only come from Jesus Christ. And he has given us the love within which to use our spiritual gifts.

Do you sense your need for Jesus in a new way?

What is done in love lasts. In other words, what is done in Christ will last. When we are serving in the name of Christ, we are serving in love. The tasks we do are not as important to God as the heart in which we do them. The biblical relationship between your spiritual gifts and your love is foundational to your understanding of ministry. You must not only reflect your passion, spiritual gifts, and personal style, but you must also express them in love.

## A Heart Condition

While the prisoners and the students whom I mentioned at the beginning of this chapter were both picking up trash, they had different motivations. The conditions of their hearts were quite different. The students demonstrated a heart of servanthood (serving with love). The prisoners seemed to have a spirit of servility (serving without love). They may or may not look the same on the outside, but within the human heart, servanthood and servility amount to two very different things.

*Servility serves out of obligation; servanthood serves out of obedience.* Servility has an "I-have-to" attitude. It feels an obligation to perform. Servanthood has an "I want to serve" spirit, and those who possess it have a heart's desire to give to others what Jesus Christ has given to them.

*Servility is being motivated to serve by what others see; servanthood is motivated by what God sees.* In servility, we are driven by a concern about what others will say or do if we don't serve, or if we don't serve in that ministry, or if we don't serve in this position, or if we don't commit a certain amount of time. The conditions can go on and on.

Servanthood is motivated by the fellowship we have with God as we serve others. Servanthood understands that ultimately we have an audience of One. It is what God sees that matters, and he sees everything.

*Servility says, "It's not my job"; servanthood says, "Whatever it takes."* When you serve with servility, you do the minimum. You accomplish only whatever is needed to get by, to fulfill the basic requirements of the task at hand. Servanthood, however, is willingness to go the extra mile; it feels the freedom to carry on beyond the job description.

Our church is intentional about having people visit our weekend services. We want to offer them a comfortable environment to hear the comforting, but uncomfortably convicting message of Jesus Christ. As a church, we work hard to take away any excuses that visitors might have for not coming back to further explore a relationship with Christ.

On one particular weekend, Dave walked into the men's restroom between the services and noticed that someone had splashed water onto the mirror. While drying his hands, he observed several paper towels and pieces of paper on the floor around the trash can. As he left, he tried to figure out who he should tell about cleaning up the restroom. It was obvious that someone wasn't doing his job.

A few minutes later, Justin walked in and noticed the same situation. He was thinking that a visitor might get the wrong impression about how they cared for God, their guests, and their facilities. Justin quickly dried off the mirror, picked up the paper towels, and walked out.

Justin was willing to do whatever it took, even if it meant going outside his "responsibilities" (servanthood). Dave, on the other hand, walked away thinking, "It's not my job" (servility).

*Servility has a ministry mind-set that says me first; servanthood has a ministry mind-set that says Father first.* Servility has its own agenda, and the goal of that agenda is to serve my needs first. Servility evaluates its involvement by asking, "What's in it for me?"

Servanthood looks up and says, "Lord, what do you have for me to do today?" It seeks the Father's agenda. Those who demonstrate servanthood have not forgotten that they have asked Jesus Christ to be Lord of their life, and they want to advance his agenda—not their own.

*Servility can have a kind of false humility or arrogance; servanthood has an authentic humility and godly pride.* Servility may take the form of saying, "Oh, God couldn't use me ... I have nothing to offer." Not true! It sounds like one is being humble, but what is really being demonstrated is false humility. Servility may go the other way and take on the form of arrogance, concerning itself with being recognized and rewarded by others. While it will happen in different ways, there is a dominating presence of "I" and "look at me."

Servanthood has a clear understanding that God has given us his Holy Spirit, spiritual gifts, and his agenda for the needs he wants us to meet on his behalf. It is God who is at work through us. This understanding makes us both humble that we can serve the living God and proud that he chooses to work through us.

*Servility is self-seeking and without permanent results; servanthood is God-glorifying and has everlasting results.* The end result of servility is a self-seeking ministry that only draws attention to the individual and his or her desire for personal gain. Servanthood results in a truly God-glorifying ministry where Jesus Christ is being honored and the focus is on a kingdom gain.

Jesus said, "Let your light shine before men, that they may see your good deeds and praise [glorify] your Father in heaven" (Matthew 5:16). We are to do visible ministry. It is okay for people to see our service! But what they see should be our serving in such a way that the love we have for each other causes them to look upward and say, "There must be a God. Look at how these people love one another!"

The religious leaders in Jesus' time went out in public parading their spirituality with holier-than-thou attitudes and practices. People could not see God in them, they could only see the Pharisees themselves. Because they lacked authentic love, most of their deeds were done in servility.

So, what about you? What is your motivation for serving? How are you doing in each of these areas? Take a minute to reflect and indicate where your heart is most of the time. And let's be honest—there is a little servility in all of us!

1. I serve **out of obligation** . . . . . . **out of obedience.**

|  | Seldom | | Sometimes | | Always |
|---|---|---|---|---|---|
|  | 1 | 2 | 3 | 4 | 5 |

2. I care about **what others see** . . . . . . **what God sees.**

|  | Seldom | | Sometimes | | Always |
|---|---|---|---|---|---|
|  | 1 | 2 | 3 | 4 | 5 |

3. My attitude is **"It's not my job."** . . . . . . **"Whatever it takes."**

|  | Seldom | | Sometimes | | Always |
|---|---|---|---|---|---|
|  | 1 | 2 | 3 | 4 | 5 |

4. My agenda is **Me first** . . . . . . **Father first.**

|  | Seldom | | Sometimes | | Always |
|---|---|---|---|---|---|
|  | 1 | 2 | 3 | 4 | 5 |

5. I have a spirit of **pride** . . . . . . **humility.**

|  | Seldom | | Sometimes | | Always |
|---|---|---|---|---|---|
|  | 1 | 2 | 3 | 4 | 5 |

6. My results are **self-seeking** . . . . . . **God-glorifying.**

|  | Seldom | | Sometimes | | Always |
|---|---|---|---|---|---|
|  | 1 | 2 | 3 | 4 | 5 |

The development of your servant's heart will flow out of your personal relationship with Jesus Christ. Your ministry will emerge as you become a fully-devoted follower of the Leader of your life. God will put the love in your heart to do the ministry he has called you to if you abide in him and he abides in you (John 15).

Visible servanthood is a testimony to the reality and presence of God: "By this all men will know that you are my disciples, if you love one another" (John 13:35).

## What Would Love Do?

Sometimes our attitude about servanthood is sorely tested by people who are clearly serving their own agendas. Take Rick's behavior, for example. Plans were being made for the annual spring clean-up day at the church. Drew talked to his small group about serving together, and they decided that Susan, Rochelle, Derek, and Rick would join him on Saturday. They were to meet at 8:30 A.M. for coffee and donuts with about sixty-five others from the church.

Rick wasn't there at 8:45 when everyone picked up their assignments. Drew's group worked along the edges of the church property cutting down brush and cleaning out the weeds along the fence. At about 11:30, Susan, Rochelle, Derek, and Drew were putting all the trash into bags. Then Rick showed up. The others were hot, tired, and dirty.

Rick jumped right in, stuffing the bags and lifting them into the truck. About five minutes later, the pastor came out to encourage the hard-working teams. He was impressed with Drew's group—all they had accomplished and how much better the grounds looked. The pastor said, "You've really done a fine job!"

"We were glad to help," Rick smiled humbly. Drew's group looked at Rick with surprise.

What would love do? How would love respond to Rick? What would you do? A situation like this puts to the test our ability to be like Christ. Yet these things happen nearly every day and give us ample opportunities to put God's kind of love into action, "Serve one another in love" (Galatians 5:13). God wants only from you what he has given to you: his love.

## If You Loved Him More

There was a young man who appeared to be a budding artist. Of all his works, he was most proud of his latest masterpiece—he had just completed a painting of the Last Supper. With childlike enthusiasm, he was anxious to show the piece to his friend and get his opinion. That friend was the writer Leo Tolstoy.

The day finally came when the young artist was able to present his work to the famous writer. He unveiled his rendition of the Last Supper. Breathlessly, he asked his friend, "What do you think?"

Tolstoy quietly studied the picture. He pondered every detail as the artist watched impatiently. The silence was finally broken as Tolstoy slowly pointed to the central figure. "You don't really love him," he said quietly.

The confused young man responded, "Why, that is the Lord Jesus Christ!"

"I know," said Tolstoy, "but if you loved him more, you would have painted him better."

Just as a picture is worth a thousand words, it is also true that actions speak louder than words. Most of us are not budding artists, but we *are* budding servants. We want to grow in our ability to glorify God and edify others. Yet someone else, looking at the central figure in our lives—Jesus Christ—might say, "If you loved him more, you would serve him better."

What do your actions say about your love for God? Do you give him your leftover time? Do you give him your leftover money? Do you do what you have to do to just "get by" spiritually? Is doing "enough" really enough? Have you become lukewarm and addicted to spiritual mediocrity?

God has given us his best in the life, death, and resurrection of his Son, the Lord Jesus Christ. He asks us to give him the first-fruits of all that we receive. God wants our best. He wants our hearts. He wants our talents. He wants our love.

Giving to God requires something from every one of us: sacrifice. And sacrifice means there is a cost involved. Giving God our best requires time, thought, and the resources he has provided. Examine the quality of your ministry, and remember: If we loved him more, we would serve him better.

Lord,
    I've got a lot to learn about love.
I'm more self-centered than I'd like anyone to know,
    and I'm often asking the silent question
"What's in it for me?"
    Lord, forgive my selfishness,
And begin a new work of love in my heart.
    Teach me the difference between servility
and true Christian service.
    Teach me to use my passion, my gifts, and my
    personal style for your glory.
Teach me to love you more
    so that I can serve you better.
In Jesus' name,
    Amen.

## Chapter Nine

# So What's My Next Step?

I couldn't believe my ears—I was hearing the words everyone fears the most. My doctor's voice was saying, "Bruce, you have cancer. Bone cancer."

For the three days following his grim report, I did not know if the disease was limb threatening or life threatening. My mind surged with terrible possibilities. Would I be there to walk any of my three daughters down the aisle at their weddings? Would I be able to play catch with my son? Could my wife face the financial and emotional challenges of raising four children alone?

By God's grace, that frightening episode had a happy ending. Through an unusual and somewhat experimental procedure, the cancerous tumor was removed, preserving both my leg and my life. Dozens of X-rays and examinations have taken place since then, the most significant one taking place five years after the surgery. Five years is a major milestone for cancer victims.

The usual X-rays were taken. I was assigned a room and waited for the results and the doctor. There in the examination room, I silently offered thanks for the additional years God had given me and wondered how many more there would be. As I reflected on my condition, my thoughts were interrupted as a nurse, the doctor, and his assistant entered the room.

Looking directly at me with a warm smile, the nurse asked how I had been doing since the last visit. The assistant went straight toward a pile of forms in the corner. Finding the appropriate one, he took his pen in hand and turned to the doctor, silently awaiting his diagnosis and prescription.

The doctor pulled the freshly developed X-ray of my right leg from its folder. In one fluid motion he slid it into the clip and flipped the switch on the light box. With his assistant looking over his shoulder, the doctor stared quietly, eyes fixed on the shadowy picture. He shifted back and forth from one foot to the other. His hands moved in and out of the pockets of his smock.

While still looking at the X-ray and fidgeting about (which he always did), he said, "There is no evidence of cancer. You're clear. Congratulations!" Then, before I had time to shout, "Yea, God!" he asked if I was ready for knee-replacement surgery.

As a result of the radical surgery, my right knee is bone on bone, an automatic prescription for the inevitable development of arthritis. The doctor explained that a knee replacement was a possible remedy for the pain. His question was not a complete surprise, but I was confused.

When I inquired as to why he was asking, he continued looking at the X-ray and pointed to some shaded areas, indicating the presence of advanced arthritis. He explained that if I was experiencing too much pain, it was time to replace the knee. When I told him that I was not having any pain or discomfort at all, he immediately turned off the light on the X-ray box. He said, "Okay, I've learned to treat the patient, not the X-ray."

Whom he listened to determined what he did.

It strikes me that it is much easier to read an X-ray than to read a person. People are emotional. They can be unpredictable. It would have been easy for the doctor to say I was wrong. But he listened before deciding on a course of action.

Maybe you're saying, "Nice story, Bruce, but what does all this have to do with me and my ministry?" Actually, it has a great deal to do with it. Like a sort of X-ray, you now have your servant profile, and I believe you are seeing the relationship between your passion, spiritual gifts, and personal style more clearly.

You'll soon be sharing with others what you've learned. You'll let them know how God is working in your life, and you'll explain the understanding you have about your ministry fit. Once you've communicated your insights, some of your friends and acquaintances may not agree or understand your commitment to be the fully devoted follower of Jesus Christ that God has called you to be. They may offer different suggestions as to what you should do with your life. When that happens, like the doctor, you will need to choose whose voice you will follow. If you are a wise person, you will always respect counsel, but ultimately, all final decisions are up to you.

## Spheres of Service

Finding your ministry fit is a process, and it works differently for everyone. We started the process by identifying your passion, gifts, and style. Then we talked about some ministries and possible expressions of your servant profile. Once those two matters of profile and possibilities were complete, finding your ministry fit may have been clear and simple. In fact, you might already be there.

However, you might still be searching for a proper position in which to get started. Or you may need to make a move to another ministry situation in the next few weeks or months. You could be coming to the realization that to really make your unique contribution, years of preparation lie ahead. More education or experience may be needed. God knows what it will take and when you will be ready to begin. Show God your faithfulness in the little things along the way, and you will see God's faithfulness in return. And as you pursue the area of service that captures the essence of your servant profile, take time to consider some other important factors.

How should you start serving? Should you change ministries? Are you doing all you can do? Let's consider three spheres of service in which your ministry may be found. You will probably serve in one or more of them at the same time.

### Organizational (Structured/Ongoing)

Organizational ministries are those that meet regularly (weekly, monthly) and have been organized to meet the ongoing needs within a small group, ministry team, or the larger church body.

Serving in the organizational sphere leads to meaningful relationships and accountability. Your commitment to use your spiritual gifts is tested in the trenches of ongoing ministry, where you join forces with other servants. Your regularly scheduled responsibilities will clearly require God's strength and grace.

Are you serving in the organizational sphere? How effective are you? Can you think of some organizational settings where you could use your passion, gifts, and style? What are they?

_____

_____

_____

_____

## Projects (Periodic/Short-term)

These ministry opportunities meet special needs that arise from time to time in the lives of those around us. Service is rendered until the task is completed, then the ministry team disbands.

Serving in the projects sphere stimulates greater creativity and encourages a spirit of servanthood. Just as financial giving includes both the regular tithe and special offerings, so ministry includes both regular serving (organizational) and special tasks (projects). Responding to these project-type opportunities allows you to stretch and broaden the scope of your usefulness.

Are you serving in the projects sphere now? How effective are you? Can you think of some projects where you could use your passion, gifts, and style? What are they?

_____

_____

_____

_____

## Promptings (Spontaneous/Personal)

These ministry opportunities are made available to each of us by the Holy Spirit. The Lord provides us with ways to serve in personal and spontaneous expressions of grace. God did not intend for us to serve him only when we are at the church or on a ministry team.

Serving in the promptings sphere develops your ministry in the most profound way. In this context, no organizational structure of leadership guides your expression. God-ordained opportunities present themselves naturally as you cross paths with those who need your ministry. As you obey the Spirit's promptings, you develop greater confidence in his guidance and find yourself serving in increasingly unexpected and exciting ways.

Are you serving in the promptings sphere now? How effective are you? Can you think of some promptings you've had where you could have used your passion, gifts, and style? What are (were) they?

_____

_____

_____

_____

The effective development of our passion, gifts, and style will encompass all three spheres of service: organizational, projects, and promptings. Each one provides us with lessons and insight for growth. Ministry satisfaction comes when we enjoy fruitfulness and fulfillment in each sphere. Your confidence and competence will grow when you experience a healthy and balanced expression of all three spheres. But there is another factor that will greatly affect your successful service—your level of spiritual maturity.

## Take Your Spiritual Snapshot

The Bible says that we must be born again (John 3:3) and that we will need spiritual milk (1 Peter 2:2) to grow up until we mature enough for solid food (Hebrews 5:13–14). Our life in Christ is a journey of growth in grace, and we are all at different levels of spiritual maturity.

There are some positions in ministry that would be best served by people with higher levels of growth. For instance, if you are a fairly new Christian, it would not be wise to lead an adult Bible study. That doesn't mean you should never be a study leader, it means you should wait until you're a bit more spiritually grown-up.

How grown-up are you? If you were to take a spiritual snapshot of your relationship with Jesus Christ, how would you describe yourself?

Are you a *seeker?* If so, you are gaining a better understanding of Christ and the Christian faith, but you have not yet personally trusted Jesus for the forgiveness of your sins. You are still investigating Christianity, still seeking its trustworthiness.

You may be surprised to learn that there are places you can participate if you are willing to help. Seek out those opportunities that enable you to mature in your relationship with Christ as you serve with committed Christians.

Are you a *new/young believer?* If you have recently become a Christian, you are excited and enthused about your new walk with Jesus Christ. Or perhaps you've been a Christian for a long time, but you are just now learning what Jesus meant when he promised abundant life. In either case, you need to grow further in your understanding of the basics of the Christian faith. You're in the process of learning what it means to walk daily in a personal relationship with Christ.

Are you a *stable/growing believer?* You are confident of God's faithfulness and ability to accomplish his will in your life. You are teachable and sensitive to the Spirit's leading, exhibiting the stability that comes from knowing Christ, regularly worshiping with his people, and actively pursuing a life of greater devotion.

Are you a *leading/guiding believer?* If so, you have reached a level of maturity in the faith where you are able to model faithfulness and inspire other believers. You lead by example, guiding others into a deeper understanding of what it means to walk personally with Jesus Christ.

Whatever your spiritual snapshot is at this time, it doesn't mean you'll always be the same. You are growing in your relationship with Christ,

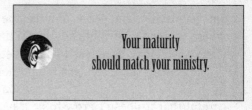

Your maturity
should match your ministry.

and these distinctions represent a minimum level of spiritual maturity needed for certain positions of responsibility.

For example, you may be a leading/guiding believer serving in an usher position that requires a minimum new/young believer level of maturity. The level of your spiritual maturity along with your servant profile will assist you in finding the best place for you to serve at this time.

## Seasons of Service

Responsibilities we have at the various stages of life also affect the seasons of our service. We shouldn't fail to be faithful to our calling, but we may not always have the same level of intensity and availability throughout the various seasons of our lives.

There are seasons where your sphere and focus of ministry will change. God is not surprised by this, and he knows you need to honor life's realities. In one season, you might be getting married. In another you could be having children. You may be in the process of divorce, being single, being a stay-at-home mom, grieving a death in the family, being a single parent, or

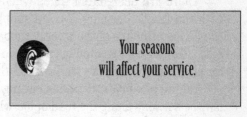

Your seasons
will affect your service.

facing a family move. All these factors need to be considered as you assess where and how to serve.

Your participation in the marketplace may also impact the nature of your involvement. You could be dealing with rotating days off, business travel, seasonal demands, or unemployment. These require you to make choices not only about how you will serve but also about how you will balance your life. Just as you need to physically eat, rest, and exercise, you need to *spiritually* eat, fellowship, and serve. You may be at a place in your career where you can contribute additional time and resources for ministry, or you may have less to offer. Let God lead. You follow.

Of course, there can be a temptation to let the seasons of life keep us from serving at all. A season may be a reason, but be careful that it doesn't grow to be a pattern. Just as work is not optional, neither is ministry service, and it should not be the first activity cut from a busy schedule.

We are all busy. We make choices. When we fail to be a regular participant in the work of ministry, we can be deceived into thinking that we are not really needed. The fact is, each of us is a part of the body of Christ and has an invaluable contribution to make. While your contribution may vary with the seasons of your life, be listening to the Holy Spirit for what it means to be a wise steward of your family relationships, marketplace responsibilities, and ministry contributions.

This doesn't mean we should never stop serving, no matter what. There are recognized times and seasons in the Bible when God's people are told to do nothing. In fact, he set the example himself: "He [God] rested on the seventh day from all His work which He had done. Then God blessed the seventh day" (Genesis 2:2–3 NASB).

There are designated times when we are supposed to rest, with the Lord's blessing. We are simply to "be" with him, not to "do." This principle of the weekly sabbath was made for us (Mark 2:27). God also instructed his people to sow and harvest the fields for six years and let the land rest on the seventh year.

Taking a sabbatical means setting aside time for rest. There may be seasons along the road of life when we need to take a serving sabbatical. Talk to your ministry leaders and those who know you well. If God is calling you to such a time, it will be confirmed by those around you. This is not time to be filled or exchanged with other activities; it is for reflection, rest, and renewal.

## The Matter of Availability

Although we are all working with different passions, gifts, styles, maturity levels, and seasons of life, each of us has the same amount of time each day—twenty-four hours. No amount of spiritual maturity, education, experience, or fame can change that. Usually, "having" time really means "making" time, and most of us are constantly making choices. When we say yes to one opportunity, we are saying no to many other possibilities. Here are some words to the wise:

> Therefore be careful how you walk, not as unwise men, but as wise, making the most of your time, because the days are evil. So then do not be foolish, but understand what the will of the Lord is. (Ephesians 5:15–17 NASB)

Just as your checkbook reveals your financial priorities and life values, your date book will indicate your spiritual priorities and life values. What kind of time does the most significant relationship in your life require? Are you spending time with God, and are you available to serve him as he is calling you—really?

I am busy, but if you called with some tickets to a basketball game, you'd be amazed at how quickly my schedule could be freed up. Many men and women say that in their hearts they would like to serve, but they really don't have much time. The fact is, it's enthusiasm that is lacking. "Sorry, I don't have time" is a typical response from someone who has not found a ministry opportunity that captures the essence of his or her passion. It is given by those who have never used their spiritual gifts or received any affirmation from the use of those gifts.

Ministering in response to your servant profile always demands time, but the necessary adjustments to your schedule will flow naturally out of obedience to the Lord's design and purpose for your life. It may not happen this week or this month. But I hope, when the time arrives, that you are willing to make the kind of schedule changes necessary to serve in the ministry God has prepared for you.

A national Gallup poll survey on volunteerism in America reported that the average volunteer serves about four to five hours a week. This includes all volunteers: believers and nonbelievers, community service groups and churches. While this is noteworthy, be careful not to use the average as your standard.

We do not dare to classify or compare ourselves with some who commend themselves. When they measure themselves by themselves and compare themselves with themselves, they are not wise. (2 Corinthians 10:12)

The real question is: How many hours are you committing to the expression of your servant profile? Would the Lord be calling you to increase those hours? To decrease them? Obedience to Jesus is our standard. Doing more or less than someone else doesn't matter. Obeying God's voice does matter.

What commitments have you made with your time? List them.

| Commitment | Hours per Week |
|---|---|
| 1. _____ | _____ |
| 2. _____ | _____ |
| 3. _____ | _____ |
| 4. _____ | _____ |
| 5. _____ | _____ |
| 6. _____ | _____ |
| 7. _____ | _____ |
| 8. _____ | _____ |
| 9. _____ | _____ |
| 10. _____ | _____ |

Now look over your list and prioritize your commitments. Are you giving to each one an appropriate amount of time? What steps might you take to be available for the things that are most important to you and to God? List a few of them.

| Priority | Steps |
|---|---|
| 1. _____ | _____ |
| 2. _____ | _____ |
| 3. _____ | _____ |

## Transitions

Finding your ministry fit is a process, and getting properly connected to the place where you are making your unique contribution takes time. It may also mean making relational and career adjustments. As you consider entering or leaving one ministry or another, you should do so with truth and grace.

First of all, when exploring a new ministry, ask the following questions:

- What are the relational expectations for you, the team, and those being served?
- How will you be trained?
- Who will provide oversight and feedback?
- What is the purpose of the ministry, and how does it relate to the overall mission of the church?
- What kind of time requirements are there, including meetings, preparation, and follow-up?
- Are there resources available for you to fulfill your ministry responsibilities?

Spend some time with those with whom you would be serving. Does the thought of spending more time with them encourage you? If not, please reconsider.

## Honor the Process

When leaving a ministry, do so without leaving unresolved issues. Communicate with your ministry leader the real reasons for your leaving. Most likely the reasons will fall within three categories: ministry fit, relational, and seasonal.

Problems with your ministry fit are inevitable when your passion, spiritual gifts, or personal style are not being affirmed or properly utilized. Feedback from your ministry will help you to grow in your understanding of your ministry fit. In whatever way problems may come to your attention, process them in an honorable way with God, ministry leaders, and trusted friends.

We all need to be committed to doing our best. A good ministry fit will result in our being fruitful and fulfilled. It is good to do a careful assessment once in a while, and if there are problems, take time to talk to your ministry leader. Are you are feeling unfruitful or unfulfilled? Consider the following:

- If you do not have emotional energy for the ministry, examine your passion.
- If you are not being effective and seeing results, examine the use of your spiritual gifts.
- If your role consistently drains you because of the position in which you serve, examine your personal style.

Dealing with these issues may lead to changes that resolve your concerns, and you won't need to leave the ministry. Or a change may be appropriate through some healthy interaction and mutual learning among you, the leader, and the ministry. God brings people to a ministry, and he sends them out from a ministry. If the truth is spoken in love, each individual will be valued, each contribution appreciated, and the ministry of the church will be enhanced.

## Facing Difficult Relationships

Sometimes a ministry change may be necessary for relational reasons. Most Christians know this, but they don't want to say it because it sounds so unloving. The truth is, it may be the loving thing to do. Having love and mutual respect for all people is not optional. Everyone is made in God's image and is to be valued. But sometimes human dysfunction, sin, and stubbornness make it too difficult for positive ministry to occur. In cases such as these, for the sake of unity, grace needs to be extended, and people should be given freedom to serve in a more harmonious environment.

Leaving a ministry is not supposed to be a quick fix, nor should it be used as an excuse for not developing our character. God will bring different kinds of people into our lives to shape us, and each relationship produces sensitivity and understanding. However, if constant tension hinders the effectiveness of the ministry, biblical steps need to be taken for resolution to take place. Here's what Jesus said: "If you are offering your gift at the altar and there remember that your brother has something against you, leave your gift there in front of the altar. First go and be reconciled to your brother; then come and offer your gift" (Matthew 5:23–24).

God is more concerned about our being at peace with one another than he is about receiving our gifts. He desires obedience more than sacrifice. "As far as it depends on you, live at peace with everyone" (Romans 12:18). Sometimes you have to go the extra distance in order to do so:

> If your brother sins against you, go and show him his fault, just between the two of you. If he listens to you, you have won your brother over. But if he will not listen, take one or two others along, so that "every matter may be established by the testimony of two or three witnesses." If he refuses to listen to them, tell it to the church; and if he refuses to listen even to the church, treat him as you would a pagan or tax collector. (Matthew 18:15–17)

While this passage is specifically talking about dealing with sinful behavior, the principle has application to the resolution of any type of behavioral or relational conflict. Obedience to these principles is our path to peace and the resolution of differences. If peace is not the result, don't destroy the body of Christ. Seek affinity with those in another ministry. Do all you can do to pursue relational oneness. "Finally, all of you, live in harmony with one another" (1 Peter 3:8).

If you need to make a ministry change for any seasonal reason, provide your leaders with adequate time to work out the transition. Change is not a sign of failure! Sometimes God orchestrates changes in order to provide new opportunities for others to serve, or to move ministries in new directions. Jesus is the head of the church. It is his body. Trust him to work in the lives of his people through the passions of their hearts, with the gifts of the Spirit, according to their personal styles. Remember to honor the process as well as the movement of the Holy Spirit in your life and ministry.

## How Are You Doing?

We've considered some of the variables that frequently enhance or inhibit ministry in general. Now let's look at your specific situation. Your ministry should be the natural outgrowth of who God made you to be. The following exercise is designed to assist you if you are already serving and are wondering whether your ministry fit is appropriate. Examine your ministry and assess its effectiveness. Respond to the following sets of questions by circling the number that best characterizes where you are in each area.

## Passion

Does your ministry reflect your passion? What need is of ultimate importance to you? Does your ministry in some way address this need?

Not Suited          Perfectly Suited
1   2   3   4   5   6   7   8   9   10

## Giftedness

Does your ministry flow out of your giftedness? Do you have the spiritual gifts needed to fulfill your ministry responsibilities? Do your ministry responsibilities stretch your gifts to their fullest potential?

Not Suited          Perfectly Suited
1   2   3   4   5   6   7   8   9   10

## Relational

Are you receiving relational affirmation? Do your coworkers within the ministry verbally affirm your contribution? Does leadership? Is there a curious silence from these people about your service?

Not Suited          Perfectly Suited
1   2   3   4   5   6   7   8   9   10

## Ministry

Are you receiving ministry affirmation? Are you being fruitful? Are you seeing results? Are those you are serving being encouraged and challenged?

Not Suited          Perfectly Suited
1   2   3   4   5   6   7   8   9   10

## Personal

Are you receiving personal affirmation? Are you feeling fulfilled? Is your esteem healthier? Do you feel better about yourself after serving in this ministry?

Not Suited            Perfectly Suited

1  2  3  4  5  6  7  8  9  10

Total your score by adding the number you circled in each of the five areas above.

*Total* _____

Consider the following interpretation:

| | |
|---|---|
| 45–50 | You are serving properly |
| 38–44 | You are probably in the right ministry (but may need more serving experience) |
| 30–37 | Some ministry changes are necessary |
| 30 or less | Seek counsel regarding a ministry that would be more in line with who God made you to be. Discuss this with your ministry leader(s). |

Whenever you are evaluating your ministry effectiveness, remember: You are not the wrong person. You are the right person, but may be in the wrong position.

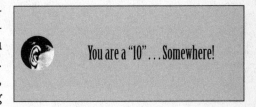

You are a "10" . . . Somewhere!

Lord,
Thank you for ongoing ministry opportunities,
   thank you for the short-term projects,
and thank you for those wonderful, spontaneous
   moments
   when you use me in some powerful and surprising way.
As I seek to grow in grace and in service,
   show me my strengths as well as my weaknesses.
Give me courage to ask questions,
   willingness to listen,
and humility to put myself under the authority of others.
   Most of all, bless my efforts.
Make much out of little,
   and turn my weakness into strength,
so you will receive the honor and glory.
   In Jesus' name,
Amen.

## Chapter Ten

# Pull Up Stakes and Follow Him!

It was 11:00 P.M. one Friday night. My friend Bobb Biehl was sound asleep when the phone rang. On the other end was Duane Pederson, founder of the *Hollywood Free Paper* and president of Duane Pederson Ministries. "Bobb," he asked, "how would you like to go to Tucson tomorrow?"

"Tucson?" Bobb groaned, "What in the world would we do in Tucson?"

"Bobby Yerkes has a circus playing in Tucson tomorrow, and I'd like to go down there, get away, clear out the cobwebs, and work the circus with him. We'll move some props, have a good time, and be back by ten o'clock tomorrow night."

Now there probably isn't a man alive who hasn't dreamed about running away with the circus as a child, so it didn't take Bobb long to agree to go.

The next morning at seven o'clock the jet lifted off the runway at Los Angeles International Airport, headed for Tucson. When Bobb and Duane got there, it was a hot, windy day at the fairgrounds where the circus was playing.

They moved props from one of the three rings to the next, helped in any way they could, and generally got dusty, dirty, tired, and hungry. During one of the breaks, Bobb started chatting with the man who trains the animals for Hollywood movies. "How is it," he asked, "that you can stake down a ten-ton elephant with the same size stake that you use for this little fellow?" (The "little fellow" weighed about three hundred pounds.)

The trainer answered with a smile, "It's easy when you know two things: elephants really do have great memories, but they really aren't very smart. When they are babies, we stake them down. They try to tug away from the stake maybe ten thousand times before they realize that they can't possibly get away. At that point, their elephant memory takes over, and they remember for the rest of their lives that they can't get away from the stake."

In some ways, we humans are like elephants. As children, we may hear that we aren't very smart, or that we are clumsy or a slob. Or, maybe as a teenager someone said about us, "He's not very handsome" or "She's not very pretty" or "They're not very good leaders," and ZAP! our minds drive a metal stake into the ground. Often, even though we are adults, we are still held back by some inaccurate one-sentence "stake" that was hammered into our minds when we were years younger. Those stakes have limited our self-understanding and image.

Today, as adults, we are capable of much more than we realize. We are able, with God's help, to pull out some of the stakes that continue to hold us back. Jesus is calling us to be what he sees in us; what he created us to be. His voice is the one that can make us free to be all we were meant to be. In Christ, we are no longer bound to the limiting stakes that others have placed in our lives. "If the Son sets you free, you will be free indeed" (John 8:36).

Through Jesus Christ and the ministry he has purposed for you, your church can be a place where stakes are pulled out of the ground and people are set free, one at a time. Jesus did not die to make us good; he died to make us free (Galatians 5:1; Romans 8:1–3). Some of us are trying to be good, but we are not free, so we are living and growing but limited by the stakes in the ground. While we attempt to do the right things, we lack joy and power. But those who are *truly* free are evidencing the goodness of God.

## Being with Jesus

Jesus raised a man named Lazarus from the dead. Standing in front of the tomb, Jesus gave three commands. He said to those around him, "Take away the stone." They did.

Jesus spoke to the man who had been dead for days, "Lazarus, come out!" He did.

Then Jesus said to the crowd that was there, "Take off the grave clothes and let him go." They did.

Jesus uses others to remove obstacles and to provide opportunities for us to hear his voice. When he calls us to experience life, we need to obey and come out of our darkness and lifeless existence into the light. But even after Lazarus was alive, he still was not free. He needed the help of those who were with Jesus to experience freedom. He needed the church!

If you and I are "with Jesus," our ministry will entail removing the obstacles that hinder people from hearing his voice and unwrapping the grave clothes (pulling up the stakes) that keep them from experiencing the fullness of Christ's freedom. We need to work together, each one fulfilling his or her specific assignments.

## A Key Question

A friend recently asked me this question, "Why are you doing what others can do, when you are leaving undone what only you can do?" This question has never left my mind. It is penetrating and cuts to the core of one's purpose. How would you answer that question?

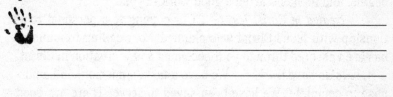

As I answer the question, my purpose is brought into focus and my commitments get prioritized. My response to this question is what gives me the power to say yes and the freedom to say no.

## Your Guarantee

God has made you a promise. He has not only designed and created you with a purpose, he has made a commitment to be with you along the way.

Being confident of this, that he who began a good work in you will carry it on to completion until the day of Christ Jesus. (Philippians 1:6)

And surely I [Jesus] am with you always, to the very end of the age. (Matthew 28:20)

God is not a quitter. If he started something, you can know with certainty he will complete it. God began a work in you and he will finish it, "because God has said, 'Never will I leave you; never will I forsake you'" (Hebrews 13:5). That's his promise. That's your guarantee!

God's intention for your life and ministry was established before the beginning of time. Your life is a part of the divine design set forth by God himself. Consider how the pieces come together in Ephesians 2:10: "For we are God's workmanship, created in Christ Jesus to do good works, which God prepared in advance for us to do." Each set of words is filled with meaning.

*We are God's workmanship* ... In the present tense, this means that God is constantly at work, actively involved in developing our daily lives and ministries. God did not wind us up and let us go. He is with us every step of the way. He finishes what he begins, and he has started a good work in you.

... *created in Christ Jesus* ... Our coming to a personal relationship with Jesus Christ was planned. Your calling to ministry has been assured through your becoming a new creation in Christ.

... *to do good works* ... We have a task, a mission, and a purpose to complete. We have been saved to serve. There are good works that God intends us to do. We cannot find the fulfillment we seek apart from the active participation of our lives in pursuit of these divine works specifically set aside for us. There are ministry contributions that only you have been designed to make.

... *which God prepared in advance* ... God's thoughtful attention to who we are and what he has planned for us is clearly demonstrated. His plans for you are specific and carefully reflect your role in his unique creation.

... *for us to do* ... God has prepared the work. He calls us to obedience. Are you prepared in your heart to do it?

Let's step back for a moment to get God's perspective. Before all of creation, God prepared some ministry opportunities for you to do: God created you; he sent Jesus Christ to make a relationship possible; he calls you; he saves you; he gives you his Holy Spirit; he places a passion in your heart; he gives you a spiritual gift; he gives you the power to use that gift; he gives you a personal style; he identifies the works he wants you to do; and he promises his continued presence.

Is there anything else God could do?

What's left to do? Simply obey!

## A Fully Devoted Follower

Matthew records the first words Jesus said to Peter: "Follow me" (Matthew 4:18–20). John records the last words Jesus said to Peter: "Follow me" (John 21:18–22). Three years of life and ministry filled the gap between these twin exhortations. Those years taught Peter invaluable lessons about power, truth, failure, and restoration.

*Peter saw power.* He saw the hungry eat, the blind made to see, the lame walk, the winds calmed, and evil flee. Following Jesus, Peter saw remarkable manifestations of power.

*Peter learned truth.* He heard truth humble the proud, uplift the brokenhearted, strengthen the doubtful, straighten the crooked, and illumine the darkness. Following Jesus, Peter learned about the transformational impact of truth.

*Peter felt failure.* He chose his own agenda instead of God's, denied Christ when he should have stood by his side, and acted impulsively rather than wisely. Following Jesus, Peter felt the disheartening weight of failure.

*Peter experienced restoration.* In spite of Peter's failures, Jesus continued to walk with him. He kept loving him; revealed to him more of his power and truth; and forgave Peter's confusion, weakness, and lack of direction. Jesus believed that a fisherman could become a fisher of men. Jesus, believing in Peter said, "And I tell you that you are Peter, and on this rock I will build my church ..." (Matthew 16:18). Following Jesus, Peter experienced the empowering joy of restoration.

For you, as for Peter, following Jesus will be a revelation of power, truth, failure, and restoration. God never gives up on his children. He is committed to you. He has called you. He is always drawing near to you and saying, "Follow me."

## Be Who You Are

When Jesus concluded his challenge to Peter to follow him, Peter looked around and pointed to another follower of Jesus and said, "Lord, what about him?" Jesus answered, "What is that to you? *You* must follow me" (John 21:21–22, emphasis mine).

You are called to follow him, and your standard of service is not what others do, but what Christ has called you to do. Whether you are doing more or less than others is not the issue. Your primary concern should be, "Are you following Christ?" Are you being obedient to his voice in your life? Are you doing what you do best in the body of Christ? He is your standard. He alone is your judge. When all is said and done, you serve an audience of One: Jesus. Will you follow him?

Lord,
    Yes, Lord. I will follow you.
Thank you for preparing good works
    for me to do,
and for equipping me to do them
    with passion, spiritual gifts, and
my own unique expression.
    Now it's time for action, Lord.
Thank you for inspiring me,
    for empowering me,
for promising to complete the good work
    you've begun in me,
and for being my unchanging Friend—
    yesterday, today and forever.
In Jesus' name,
    Amen.

# A Word to Leaders

An officer reported to General Marshall during World War II with the news that a commander in the field was incompetent. He wanted to know what to do. The general gave an order to have the commander removed immediately. Quickly the officer came back with, "But who will replace him?"

General Marshall looked straight at the officer and firmly said, "Who we get to replace him is the second issue. Our first responsibility is to fulfill the trust given to us by the government, families, and the soldiers under his command. We cannot let someone known to be incompetent remain in their position."

General Marshall went on to say, "The fact that the commander is not competent for the position is not so much a criticism of the individual as it is of the leaders who placed him there." He concluded with, "It is now our responsibility to find where that commander is competent and put him there."

## Who Is Responsible?

Let's be honest. Speaking leader to leader, we have recruited people to serve and then criticized them for not performing well. Oftentimes we did not train them. In many instances we did not give them adequate feedback. It is very likely, and maybe even probable that we never took the time to ask them if and how God might be leading them to serve. Let's face it, we had some slots to fill, and all we were looking for were some people with a pulse who were warm and willing. And that may be just what we got. Then we complain that people are just not committed, because if they were, they would surely take responsibility for their (our) ministry.

The fact that they are incompetent for the ministry we have assigned them is, in reality, a commentary on us as leaders. The pressures of ministry have caused many of us to launch ahead prematurely, not understanding our people and/or what we are requiring of them.

But expectations have changed. The wind of the Spirit is shifting us back to the biblical community the church was designed to be. More than ever before, God's people are open, desirous, and in some cases even demanding their role within the ministry of the church and the marketplace. In increasing numbers, believers who are entering midlife are viewing their personal crisis as life's half-time, where plans are being put into place for the second half. These plans involve some of the kingdom's high-capacity, high-caliber, marketplace leaders who are committed to moving from success to significance.

As a leader in the church, are you ready to guide and utilize these resources?

Since the Reformation, we have been talking about the priesthood of all believers. Congregations are getting tired of talking. They want action. They want help to grow in their understanding of how to be faithful to their ministry (if they only knew what it was). Can you provide them with the leadership they need?

## A Time of Changing Roles

It is a new day. God is putting his ministry into the hands of all his people, not just those who are ordained. You know what that means, don't you? That's right, your role as a pastor or ministry leader is changing as a result of the increased self-understanding of the believer. As their expectations increase for ministry, what they need and are coming to expect from you as a leader is different than what it has been in the past. Have you noticed that in recent years?

The winds are becoming gusty. With each passing year, your effectiveness as a leader will be assessed more and more by your ability to identify, attract, and lead teams of unpaid staff (lay people, volunteers). It has been said, "We need to illuminate the laity," meaning we must help each believer to rise up to their rightful and priestly roles. We are all priests. We are all ministers with a ministry.

Don't be caught unaware. I foresee in the next twenty years many leaders who are going to be sidelined because they did not notice the wind shifting, or because they failed to make the personal and leadership adjustments necessary to remain competent to lead the church in the twenty-first century. Many know; few learn. I visit constantly with leaders who have read the books, know the language, and preach it consistently, but who are failing to put their theology into practice.

On the other hand, sometimes it is the congregation who wants the safety of the paid professional to do the ministry, while they help out once in awhile. They do not understand their call and are certainly not walking worthy of it. Historically, we are enjoying a window of opportunity that is unprecedented, that requires us to take action. I hope you share my sense of urgency.

Can you imagine a church where everyone is serving according to their God-given passion, spiritual gifts, and personal style with a servant's heart? You could not keep the world away from such demonstrations of love. Those who say it can't be done need to get out of the way of those who are doing it, because more and more churches are doing it! As the cloud led God's people in the desert, his Spirit is leading God's people today. He is taking us into a new land of full participation within the body of Christ. Will you stay behind, or will you come along and provide some leadership?

The speed of the leader determines the speed of the team. Seek to understand how your church can facilitate and enhance the ministries of God's people. It must start with *you*. Have you done a careful, personal assessment of your own passion, spiritual gifts, and style? Is your ministry reflecting your servant profile? Do you need to make some adjustments in your ministry responsibilities? What is Jesus saying to you?

You don't have to have all the answers—just a willingness to walk with the leaders of your church to identify their profiles and develop an ongoing approach to do the same with your congregation. Look at the available resources and attend those training opportunities that will best meet the needs of your church.

We are all in this together, but each of us must do our part!

# Network:
# The Right People...
# In the Right Places...
# For the Right Reasons!

*What You Do Best* provides the vision and values for a comprehensive and repeatable identification and placement process known as *Network*. It has been designed for local churches and ministry organizations to guide their people. *Network*'s discovery sessions are where people identify their passion, spiritual gifts, and personal style through the use of teaching, overheads, videos, assessments, and huddle-group interaction.

*Network*'s goal is service. It does not stop with the individual's identification, but through a one-on-one consultation each believer is assisted in finding specific ministry positions where they could serve according to their servant profile. A complete implementation guide details each essential step in the creation of ministry-position descriptions, staff training, and ministry development. *Network* is a people-flow management system for the church.

The *Network* materials are biblically based and have been designed so that the average church will have above-average results. All the forms, guides, and materials you need to start your own *Network* ministry are available to you. Coauthored by Bruce Bugbee, Don Cousins, and Bill Hybels, these materials were developed in thousands of successful applications at Willow Creek Community Church and in other churches and regions.

Leaders of churches who already use the *Network* process are firmly convinced of its effectiveness (see Appendix 3). They point to such factors as increased membership, increased volunteerism, increased giving, reduced ministry turnover, and overall, greater ministry satisfaction.

*Network* can help your church get the right people in the right places for the right reasons. Your leadership will be enhanced through *Network*'s repeatable, proven process to consistently place motivated believers into meaningful places of service. *Network* provides you with the practical implementation tools needed to lead your people into ministry responsibilities where they can be fruitful and fulfilled.

Leaders who are implementing *Network* are also experiencing greater personal and organizational effectiveness and are able to meet more needs in their church and community. These leaders are enjoying an increased enthusiasm for ministry and a renewed vision for the mission of the church. Will you join them?

Call 1-800-588-8833 today for     ... a Network kit
                                               ... Network University Training
                                               ... Database support
                                               ... other resources and information

**Network Curriculum Kit**               (0-310-50109-1)      $159.99 ea
*Includes items marked with ***

**Network Participant's Guide***       (0-310-41231-5)      $10.99 ea.
*A superb workbook for your people to follow through the sessions.*

**Network Consultant's Guide***        0-310-41231-5)      $10.99 ea.
*A guide for you and other leaders to use in connecting Network participants to actual positions of service in your church.*

**Network Implementation Guide***     0-310-43261-8)      $24.99 ea.
*Shows you in clear, step-by-step fashion how to set up the program.*

**Network Leader's Guide***        (0-310-41241-2)     $29.99 ea.
*Designed for you or whoever actually trains your people.*

**Network Drama Vignettes Video***   (0-310-41189-0)     $24.99 ea.
*An excellent teaching tool that brings key concepts brilliantly to life.*

**Network Vision and Consultant**
   **Training Video***            (0-310-24499-4)     $24.99 ea.
*An exciting overview of the program which will help others grasp the full potential of the Network idea for your congregation! The video also includes a reenactment of the consultation process.*

**Network Overhead Masters***      (0-310-48528-2)     $19.99 ea.
*Fully produced and professionally designed, for use in the Discovery Sessions.*

**Network Audio Pages**             (0-310-41188-2)     $12.99 ea.
   **Volume I (2 cassettes) Discovery Sessions 1–4.**

**Network Audio Pages**             (0-310-24498-6)     $12.99 ea.
   **Volume II (2 cassettes) Discovery Sessions 5–8.**
*The complete Discovery Sessions as taught by Bruce Bugbee (not included in Network Kit).*

For a training schedule, conference list, newsletter, or a current list of available resources, call, write, fax, or e-mail:

**Network Ministries International**
27355 Betanzos
Mission Viejo, CA 92692
Phone: 800–588–8833
Fax: 714–854–1268
E-mail: NetMin@AOL.com

**Willow Creek Association**
P.O. Box 3188
Barrington, IL 60011–3188
Phone: 708–765–0070
Fax: 708–765–5046

# One Life at a Time... One Church at a Time

The following are actual letters from churches who have implemented the principles of *What You Do Best* through the *Network* program.

## Solutions

Dear Network Ministries International,

Good music will get people to visit your church. Good preaching will get them to stay six months, maybe a year. But, unless people become plugged in and begin developing a sense of ownership in the church, they won't stick. It's easy to state the problem, much harder to come up with a solution.

The Network process has been an important part of the solution at Christ Community Church. After using Network for the past five years, we have seen an explosion of ministry in our church. Not only has the number of people serving in our church grown by leaps and bounds, but their impact has dramatically increased.

It's been exciting to watch the "ripple effect" of Network spread throughout the church. Network has impacted . . .

- Assimilation: People who serve, stay.
- Unity: People who are busy and fulfilled in ministry don't have time to sweat the small stuff.
- Giving: Attenders don't give; owners do.
- Ministry Development: The identification of gifted, passionate leaders is the first step in beginning any ministry.

Network is not another spiritual gifts seminar. People have been talking about spiritual gifts for years, but all the talk and tests haven't had much impact. Why? People get all revved up but have nowhere to go. The beauty of Network is that it is a process, easily implemented by church staff and lay people, that empowers people to use their gifts to impact the church the way God intended. Unlike so many other programs on the market, Network has not been developed by theoreticians but by practitioners who have made it work.

All I can say is Network works, at least it has at Christ Community Church. I'm excited that more and more churches are implementing Network and will see for themselves.

Craig Parker
Christ Community Church
St. Charles, Illinois

## Equipping and Empowering

Dear Friends at Network,

Mobilizing God's people to effectively use their God-given gifts is not a gimmick dreamed up by a Christian Education pastor desperate to staff programs. Rather it is God's design that will help each member of your church better understand their part of God's work in the world. At College Church, Network has excited our people to serve with greater understanding and effectiveness as they learn not only what their gifts are, but where to use them in ministry.

Network has been a logical next step for new people who have gone through our four-week orientation class. The by-product of Network is a highly motivated group of lay people who either plug into a ministry, start a ministry, or receive affirmation regarding their present service. Ministry Position Descriptions for every conceivable position in the church have helped us organize and recruit the right person for the different ministries.

As a leader, what excites me is the opportunity to open up God's Word and share the truths about spiritual gifts, but it's more than that. Through Network, we have the opportunity to share our philosophy of ministry, and that places all our volunteers on the same page!

God's mission in the work is bigger than our church, and his vision for our church is bigger than our staff. Network allows us to equip and empower our people to take their spiritual gifts and put them to work. The result is people are growing to become more like Christ and we are better able to reach His vision. Network is more than an answer to your recruiting frustrations, it is a well-thought-out approach which will allow you to couple your church's philosophy to and through the Network process. The result will be positive, I'm sure.

Marc Maillefer
College Church
Wheaton, Illinois

## Making an Individual and Organizational Impact

Dear Bruce,

The impact of Network has been phenomenal, both individually and organizationally. Many people in our church have gained by becoming more focused, appreciating other parts of the body, demonstrating a sense of true servanthood, finding their gifts and using them, and so on.

Let me tell you about a Network success. Here's what happened. One of our audio engineers is extremely "talented" as a keyboard player. I mean this guy can play any type of musical piece, TV commercial, movie theme—whatever—right out of his head. So naturally we were pushing him to play in the band. One night after a band practice I went out for a coffee with him. After a while he told me he was kind of frustrated playing in the band. Although he could play well, although he liked the other guys in the band and their level of ability, he didn't have a passion for playing keyboards in front of an audience. This frustrated him, but he wasn't sure why.

Without my exposure to Network I might have banged him over the head and somehow guilted him into playing. And I realize in retrospect that today I would still be banging him over the head, or else I might not even have had a head to bang on.

Instead, I took a deep breath and gave Network a shot. I briefly explained the Network idea and asked him, "What do you get energy out of doing?"

"Well, I like video," he said, "but I don't have much experience."

"Let's do it," I said.

Now we have a video group with other passionate persons that is led by this "keyboard player." We can't hold him down. He has so much energy for video. His enthusiasm is contagious, and people in the video group have spent up to three days a week of nonworking time on video. On occasion they have worked on video through the night, not realizing the time. We have people who have spiritually grown, and we have a very exciting video program all because God used Network. And this example is just one of many.

Additionally, our church has already acted as a Network consultant for two other area churches and promoted Network to many others. It has been a highly effective process.

Ken Byl
Hope Community Church
Surrey, British Columbia

## Making Church History

Dear Network Ministries,

We believe God is calling us to produce a distinctive kind of person, one who is fully devoted to Jesus Christ, one who is a spirit-gifted servant who meets specific human need. This is becoming central to our mission.

Since consistently teaching the Network Seminar for four years, we have witnessed

- a greater joy and passion for doing God's work
- greater awareness to care for the worker as well as the work done
- a growing base of spirit-gifted servants
- a much more diversified ministry

It's no wonder that Network has helped fuel the greatest growth period in the church's fifty-four year history.

David J. Wine
College Church of the Nazarene
Bourbonnais, Illinois

Do you have a story to tell? If so, please fax it to me at (714)854-1268 or send it to:

**Network Ministries International**
27355 Betanzos
Mission Viejo, CA 92692

# Network Ministries International

### Bruce Bugbee
*Founder and President*

Network Ministries International exists to support the ministry of the local church and Christian organizations in the effective and efficient use of God's people. It is committed to believers' serving according to their passion, spiritual gifts, and personal style, being both fruitful and fulfilled in a meaningful place of service.

Network Ministries International provides leadership training and support on the most current procedures being used for volunteer and staff identification and placement processes. Not only are seminars, tapes, and written material available, but a comprehensive training experience is provided through Network University. It brings you a faculty of experienced leaders who know what is working in today's churches. Get the training you need to support the ministry you have.

Encourage your believers. Strengthen your leaders. Implement the process that has helped hundreds of churches become more biblical communities. Call now to learn more!

Let us know how we can serve you.

For a training schedule, conference information, newsletter, or a current list of available resources, please contact:

Bruce Bugbee, Founder and President
**Network Ministries International**
PMB 217—25108 B Marguerite Parkway
Mission Viejo, CA 92692
Phone: 800–588–8833
Fax: 949-768-8076
E-mail: nmi@networkministries.com
Website: www.networkministries.com

# About the Author

Bruce Bugbee was raised in southern California in an unchurched family. After making his commitment to Christ at the age of eighteen, he participated in a number of ministries: the Crystal Cathedral (Robert Schuller), Calvary Chapel (Chuck Smith), Young Life, the Presbyterian church, the Covenant church, the Reformed church, and Willow Creek Community Church (Bill Hybels). He has experienced local church, para-church, regional, and denominational responsibilities.

Following his call into full-time ministry, Bruce pursued a major in religious studies at Westmont College in Santa Barbara, California, and a master of divinity degree at Fuller Theological Seminary in Pasadena. His emphasis is on church renewal, people development, leadership, and church administration. He has been ordained with the Reformed Church in America since 1979.

Bruce served as a youth pastor in several California churches for twelve years (1970–82) before accepting the Director of Area Youth Ministries position in the regional office of the Reformed Church located in Orange City, Iowa (1982–86). His denomina-tional and regional responsibilities included leadership training and resource development as well as camping and retreat min-istries. He directly influenced over two hundred churches in the western United States and Canada. In 1986, he became the Pas-toral Care Director and codeveloper of the *Network Ministry* at Willow Creek Community Church near Chicago, Illinois. He has also provided leadership and coordination for Willow Creek's internship program to over forty leaders and church planters.

Bruce coauthored *Network: The Right People ... In the Right Places ... For the Right Reasons* (Zondervan, 1994). This Gold-medallion winning dynamic personal study and assessment process assists believers in better understanding who God has made them to be. He has personally led over twelve thousand volunteers through the *Network* process, where they identified their passions, spiritual gifts, and personal style in order to make their unique contribution in a meaningful place of service. Another one hundred and fifty thousand believers have used *Network* in hundreds of churches around the world.

Bruce's leadership, administration, and communication gifts have made him effective in the areas of individual and ministry assessments, internship programs, and volunteer and staff identification and placement.

In June of 1993, Bruce founded Network Ministries International. Its purpose is to support the ministry of the local church and the mission of Christian organizations in the effective and efficient use of God's people for loving service to one another and the world. Assisting leaders in the development of gift-based ministries, he writes, speaks, and trains leaders through Network University and various other conferences and events.

Bruce continues his ministry in the local church on staff at South Coast Community Church (Irvine, California) as the Pastor of Ministry Development. He and his wife, Valerie, were married in 1974, and they have four children: Brittany, Brianne, Bronwyn, and Todd. They live in Mission Viejo, California.

This resource was created to serve you and to help you in building a local church that prevails! It is just one of many Willow Creek Resources copublished by the Willow Creek Association and Zondervan Publishing House.

Since 1992, the Willow Creek Association (WCA) has been linking like-minded, action-oriented churches with each other and with strategic vision, training, and resources. Now a worldwide network of over five thousand churches from more than eighty denominations, the WCA works to equip Member Churches and others with the tools needed to build prevailing churches. Our desire is to inspire, equip, and encourage Christian leaders to build biblically functioning churches that reach increasing numbers of unchurched people, not just with innovations from Willow Creek Community Church in South Barrington, Illinois, but from any church in the world that has experienced God-given breakthroughs.

## Willow Creek Conferences

In the past year, more than 65,000 local church leaders, staff, and volunteers—from WCA Member Churches and others—attended one of our conferences or training events.

Conferences offered on the Willow Creek campus in South Barrington, Illinois, include:

**Prevailing Church Conference**—Foundational training for staff and volunteers working to build a prevailing local church; offered twice each year.

**Prevailing Church Workshops**—More than fifty workshops cover seven topic areas that represent key characteristics of a prevailing church; offered twice each year.

**Promiseland Conference**—Children's ministries; infant through fifth grade.

**Prevailing Youth Ministries Conference**—Junior and senior high ministries.

**Arts Conference**—Vision and training for Christian artists using their gifts in the ministries of local churches.

**Leadership Summit**—Envisioning and equipping Christians with leadership gifts and responsibilities; broadcast live via satellite to sixteen cities.

**Contagious Evangelism Conference**—Encouragement and training for churches and church leaders who want to be strategic in reaching lost people for Christ.

**Small Groups Conference**—Exploring how small groups can play a key role in developing authentic Christian community that leads to spiritual transformation.

## Prevailing Church Regional Workshops

Each year the WCA team leads seven, two-day training events in cities across the United States. Workshops are offered in topic areas including leadership, next-generation ministries, small groups, arts and worship, evangelism, spiritual gifts, financial stewardship, and spiritual formation. These events make quality training more accessible and affordable to larger groups of staff and volunteers.

## Willow Creek Resources

Churches can look to Willow Creek Resources for a trusted channel of ministry tools in areas of leadership, evangelism, spiritual gifts, small groups, drama, contemporary music, financial stewardship, spiritual transformation, and more. For ordering information, call 800-570-9812 or visit www.willowcreek.com.

## WCA Membership

Membership in the Willow Creek Association as well as attendance at WCA Conferences is for churches, ministries, and leaders who hold to a historic, orthodox understanding of biblical Christianity. The annual church membership fee of $249 provides discounts for your entire team on all conferences and Willow Creek Resources, networking opportunities with other outreach-oriented churches, a bimonthly newsletter, a subscription to *Defining Moments* monthly audio journal, and more.

## WillowNet (www.willowcreek.com)

This internet service provides you with access to hundreds of Willow Creek messages, drama scripts, songs, videos, and multimedia suggestions. The system allows you to sort through these elements and download them for a fee.

Our website also provides detailed information on the Willow Creek Association, Willow Creek Community Church, WCA Membership, conferences, training events, resources, and more.

Willow Creek Association
P.O. Box 3188
Barrington, IL 60011-3188
Phone: 800-570-9812
Fax: 888-922-0035
Web: www.willowcreek.com